MW00773019

"Effective prison teaching requires sensitivit[...] provides a great service to instructors by sh[...] emotional contours of these spaces. This boo[...] prisons and other harshly controlled environments more effectively, for the benefit of their students and of the education programs they work with."

Rebecca Ginsburg, *Director, Education Justice Project, University of Illinois Urbana-Champaign*

"This is a seminal work in the field of education [that] addresses two factors that are not understood and overlooked in the assessment and evaluation: trauma and epistemology. This book examines the most current constructs of intergenerational trauma from epigenetics and offers solutions...European culture takes pride in the formulation of its own epistemology starting at the cradle of Western Civilization...[but] Plato realized that there was more than one way to teach and learn. We should follow his guidance."

Edwin J. Nichols, *Ph.D. Clinical/Industrial Psychologist, Author of* The Philosophical Aspects of Cultural Difference

"*Building a Trauma-Responsive Educational Practice* is a well-organized and comprehensive overview of how best to support adult students with trauma-informed approaches...What Em Daniels has done within this book has pulled together the many other ways in which trauma shows up – from the generational and systemic societal issues to the childhood traumas many people within U.S. society have. This book gives a solid introduction that is both accessible to an educated lay audience and an overview of the various types of trauma that humans experience. Em draws upon the brain science as well as the social science findings to synthesize otherwise disparate literatures that can be difficult to navigate and provided interpretation around how to apply these studies to our practices as educators.

Building a Trauma-Responsive Educational Practice is a huge contribution to the higher education literature around trauma and teaching that has, until very recently, been overlooked. Higher education practitioners will be well served by reading this book and changing up their pedagogy and practices to better serve the students they work with. I am so excited that this book exists and cannot wait to make good use of it on my campus, with the faculty and staff I serv."

Xyanthe N. Neider, *Ph.D. Director for Teaching and Learning Whatcom Community College*

"Daniels is a scholar whose inquiry is deeply informed by their decades long work as a practitioner. This book should be required reading for those hoping to enter the carceral space with the hope of doing good. Daniels approaches this work in the spirit of generosity-offering to those who will come after them-a beautiful and thoughtful roadmap"

Jessica Katz, *Founding Director of the Family Preservation Project*

"Em Daniels' *Building a Trauma-Responsive Educational Practice: Lessons from a Correction Classroom* is a call to action to transform our education system into one that is rooted in compassion and joy. As an adult educator, I appreciate the in-depth research of the connection between trauma, the brain and learning while also providing practical tools to change the classroom environment so I can be part of a much needed change in our education system. The author writes from the heart and takes you into a journey that will change the way you see and practice teaching and learning."

Caro Forero, *Educator, Seattle Central College*

"Em Daniels cracks open the gates of prison to give educators insight into best practices for teaching within correctional settings. They offer up their experience and research in order to provide a guide in teaching students who are incarcerated. Readers are given an opportunity to consider a trauma-informed approach to education that will give students who are already resilient a chance to learn in the safety of the classroom you can create within the walls of a prison."

Emily Dykstra-Jones, *Education Navigator, Washington State*

"Em Daniels has written the first comprehensive body of work asking us to examine our lived experience and epistemology (of language and treatment) around trauma in higher education. This read is must for K–12 and post-secondary education. The new foundational perspective is a solid foundation to begin to comprehend historical spheres of influence, impacted by Euro-centric values, within the work we do to support students' access, access+success, and success—as wells as ways to mitigate and restore individual and community strength."

Dr. Claudine Richardson Fraser, *Policy Associate for Washington SBCTC Student Success Center*

"Em Daniels' trauma-responsive educational space in the prison where we met is where I began to reclaim myself as a learner. If you are serious about helping people help themselves— BUY THIS BOOK! Em outlines specific strategies to help those closest to the problem survive AND grow, coming out the other side informed, empowered, and prepared to build a life worth living. Em leads by example in their work, and now in this book, I'm living proof."

Nova Sweet, *Nova Sweet, LCSW Family Preservation Project Community Lead Organizer*

"Em Daniels writes a compelling, informative, and ultimately hopeful text about teaching and learning in carceral spaces and beyond. Most educators espouse that education is transformative—learning promotes reflection, facilitates connections and leads to new possibilities for individuals. Many are proponents of providing educational opportunities for those who are imprisoned. However, little has been written or discussed about what this should look like to make the experience transformative. Context setting is the key and Daniels provides educators with an understanding of what it means to learn while imprisoned. Most importantly, they highlight the role of trauma on the learning process and provides tangible strategies for supporting and enhancing learning for students who have or are experiencing trauma. Suffice to say, many of our students have or are experiencing trauma, so Daniels ideas reach beyond carceral spaces. I look forward to applying much of what they have written into my own college classroom. This book reminds me of why I choose teaching as a profession. Teaching and learning is about relationships and facilitating growth beyond textbook knowledge. Daniels provides a heartfelt, practical, and inspiring text to help us move education forward."

Candyce Reynolds, *Ph.D. Professor, Postsecondary, Adult and Continuing Education Chair, Educational Leadership and Policy Portland State University*

"If you are an educator, administrator, leader or facilitator looking to create learning experiences based on connection, expansion and even joy, read this book and apply the principles and practices Daniels so compassionately lays out. We have a duty to no longer perpetuate systems and spaces that re-traumatize participants—this book is our call to that duty."

Building a Trauma-Responsive Educational Practice

This timely manual presents a new perspective on teaching and learning focused on countering the impacts of trauma on adults' ability to learn. Within its detailed and useful approaches, Daniels provides a road map for building a trauma-responsive teaching practice grounded in the principles of Trauma-Informed Care, and emphasizing the need for educators to develop a rigorous practice of self-care.

Prison classrooms, in particular, demonstrate the intersectional and overlapping nature of systemic, historical, and individual traumatic experience. People who rediscover themselves as learners while in corrections classrooms have a unique and powerful perspective to bring to the work of ending mass incarceration, and the role of education and learning in that ending.

The concepts and framework presented in the text aim to expand how we define "working with trauma." Through this redefinition, we better align teaching and learning as counters to the impacts of trauma. As this alignment transforms educational philosophy and practice, we have an opportunity to repurpose the nature of education itself, and shift toward learning *how* to learn.

Although this book contains content specific to corrections educators, or those aspiring to teach in prisons, its concepts and activities are applicable to any environment or situation in which adults need to learn. Adult educators, front-line personnel in any public service role, librarians, legal professionals, judges, lawyers—all can benefit from the expertise shared in this book.

Em Daniels is a master educator and leading expert in the impacts of trauma and incarceration on adult learners, adult education inside prisons, jails, and on free campuses as people transition into education after returning to their communities. Daniels is a skilled facilitator and speaker, with an extensive and varied background in adult education, instructional design, curriculum building, and program development. They hold an M.S. degree in Teaching, General Arts, and Letters, from Portland State University and a B.A. in Communications from the University of North Carolina at Charlotte.

Building a Trauma-Responsive Educational Practice

Lessons from a Corrections Classroom

Em Daniels

Routledge
Taylor & Francis Group

NEW YORK AND LONDON

Cover image: © Getty Images

First published 2022
by Routledge
605 Third Avenue, New York, NY 10158
and by Routledge

2 Park Square, Milton Park, Abingdon, Oxon, OX14 4RN
Routledge is an imprint of the Taylor & Francis Group, an informa business

© 2022 Taylor & Francis

Library of Congress Cataloguing-in-Publication Data
Names: Daniels, Em, author.
Title: Building a trauma-responsive educational practice: lessons from a corrections
classroom / Em Daniels.
Description: New York, NY : Routledge, 2022. | Includes bibliographical references and
index.
Identifiers: LCCN 2021031004 (print) | LCCN 2021031005 (ebook) | ISBN 9780367499631
(hbk) | ISBN 9780367499624 (pbk) | ISBN 9781003048312 (ebk)
Subjects: LCSH: Prisoners--Education. | Education--Philosophy. | Corrections.
Classification: LCC HV8875 .D44 2022 (print) | LCC HV8875 (ebook) | DDC 365/.661--dc23
LC record available at https://lccn.loc.gov/2021031004
LC ebook record available at https://lccn.loc.gov/2021031005

ISBN: 978-0-367-49963-1 (hbk)
ISBN: 978-0-367-49962-4 (pbk)
ISBN: 978-1-003-04831-2 (ebk)

DOI: 10.4324/9781003048312

Typeset in Bembo
by MPS Limited, Dehradun

Contents

Figures

"How are we supposed to treat others?" "There are no others."
~Ramana Maharshi

"You are not obligated to complete the work, but neither are you free to abandon it."
~the Talmud

Acknowledgments

This book did not get written in isolation. I always wondered why authors thanked so many people in the Acknowledgments and now I know—it takes so many people giving encouragement, asking a good question, or sending cheer on bad days.

This text would not be here with out my dear friend and colleague, Bill. The Trauma Responsive Framework is our co-creation and although I am writing this book, connecting trauma, adult learning, and incarceration was, and still is, a shared endeavor.

JKatz, my ride or die, you are the best friend and partner in justice I could ever have wanted. Marge, you've been with me through the thick of it and there is no way to thank you enough. Dr. Erin Corbett, none of this would have happened without you. You are a brilliant scholar and human, although Caesar might be cuter. Dr. Candyce Reynolds, you started this whole thing and have stayed with it all these years. From all of us in the Mentor room—we love you.

Mom, thank you and I love you.

Erin M., Kathy, Carmen, Xyan, Mel, Ellen, Amanda, Ambar, Emily, Hanan, Dr. Claudine Richardson, Kim —I couldn't ask for a better group of brilliant, thoughtful friends and colleagues.

Connan and Pat—thanks for trusting me and giving me room to let my Orange flag fly.

Most of all –thank you to each of my students.

Preface

When I first began thinking about teaching I was in grad school. I knew there was something about the "how" of teaching that we could be doing better, but I could not name, or even describe what I was feeling. Over the years, I have tried, over and over, to articulate this feeling, but to no end. When I left my work at the prison, I thought I wanted to write about that experience, but those attempts also fell flat. When I finally understood that I was trying to write about trauma and learning, especially in prisons and jails, I thought that was the core of this book.

It took a close friend pressing me, over and over, to continue digging into my "why," before I uncovered (two weeks before deadline) what I have always known: Learning must become an experience in joy for adults and children alike. As adults, learning itself is rarely joyful. We enjoy *doing* what we have learned, but the process itself is painful, fraught with perfectionism, imposter syndrome, shame, and doubt. Imagine a world where joy in learning is part of the process; a world where we are encouraged to seek pleasure and enjoy learning, balanced with accepting the responsibility that comes with knowledge.

The first novel I ever read was Madeine L'Engle's *A Swiftly Tilting Planet*. My third-grade teacher gave me a paperback copy and I still have it—torn and yellowed from being read dozens and dozens of times. In the story, a nondescript dog turns up at the Wallace household, a female with a golden coat and feathery tail. The family names her Ananda, a Sanskrit word meaning "that joy in existence without which the universe would collapse." I have never forgotten the idea that without joy, the universe itself would cease.

That book was my first exposure to a world of imagination and joy, reality as fantasy, and beauty and terror. Writing this book has been a constant struggle to find a way through the bleak reality of mass incarceration, grinding trauma, grieving at how firmly education and learning are enmeshed with both. I came closest to giving up when I was writing Chapter 4—how is it possible that anyone would want to work in places of such misery and harm? But millions of people live in those places, and they do not have the choice of giving up, of leaving, of turning away. We cannot abandon them, and we cannot allow their dreams and hopes to disappear from our shared consciousness.

Teachers currently working in prisons and jails are burned out and overwhelmed, frustrated with their lack of understanding and knowledge of how to best help their students. On a national scale, people in carceral spaces have been either harmed or abandoned by organized education for so long that even the thought of calling for change is daunting. But as with any problem, naming and describing is necessary before transformation can begin. Without understanding the role of organized education in furthering systemic, racial trauma, teaching in carceral spaces holds only a fraction of its potential.

The Trauma-Responsive Educational Framework is a tool educators can use to reframe how they approach their classrooms. The Expansive Learning Model imagines well-developed learning as a pathway of evolutionary possibility. But without joy, neither can be fully realized. This book is as much a call to joy in the face of despair as it is a conversation about teaching in prison, or the impacts of trauma on learning. Joy is what we can bring, no matter our circumstances, and joy in teaching is a revolution.

As our learning on the impacts of trauma increases, and the field of trauma and adult learning expands, I hope to hear this conversation grow, highlighting voices of those who have been most impacted. I believe I am presenting information in a new way, but this work is not new. Black women have been leading community settling and healing work in carceral spaces for decades, and their work has informed mine. They hold the wisdom and experience we need as we seek a way forward, into a world of mutual care and support.

Writing this book feels risky, as leaps of intuition and faith often do. But as part of this work is critiquing our dependence on Euro-white knowledge frameworks, it seems right be bold and put forth this newly sprouted idea, knowing that one person alone cannot bring it into fullness. As you think and feel through what I've written, I look forward to hearing, reading, and seeing your responses, how you plan to grow and nourish the work.

In solidarity and care,

em

Foreword

I have had the privilege of serving children and adults from marginalized and disenfranchised populations for the past 33 years in a variety of professional and para-professional roles including nearly two decades in education. Half that time was in a carceral setting, including three years as an Adult Education instructor. My undergrad work is in Education and my graduate work is in Addiction Studies. I also served time in state prison. During that time, I worked as an Education Assistant in the prison education department. I have experienced our education system both inside and outside the wire from diverse perspectives and I can only say that I wish I would have had a copy of *Building a Trauma-Responsive Educational Practice* to underpin my work as an educator.

I met Em Daniels in 2018, eight years post release. We were both working in reentry at the time. I was immediately struck by Em's authenticity and compassion as we talked about our common challenges teaching in a carceral environment. I think it was our commitment to our students that bound us in friendship and collegiality. Long story short, for the last three years, I have had the honor of co-creating and facilitating in-service trainings with Em in colleges and prison education programs on how staff can incorporate a trauma-responsive approach into their teaching approach.

One of the biggest hurdles in our work became how to disseminate all the intricacies and facets of this concept into a two-hour, four-hour, or even a two-day training. Integrating a trauma-responsive approach into the classroom is far more than the just the awareness that students have been exposed to adverse life events that interfere with their ability to learn. It is more than demonstrating unconditional positive regard and knowing how not to trigger or retraumatize students. It is a comprehensive understanding of the impact of trauma in relation to race, racial disparity, power dynamics, emotional fluency, resiliency, and a myriad of other components and concepts.

So, when Em told me she was thinking of writing a book, my first thought was, "Finally!" Educators and other student-facing staff can have a comprehensive guide to working with students impacted by trauma and especially those students who are currently or formerly incarcerated.

When I read *Building a Trauma-Responsive Educational Practice*, I knew Em had hit the mark. As far as I can tell, based on over three decades of experience working with populations at high risk of exposure to adverse life events, Em has left no stone unturned. She offers the reader a complete accounting of the vast, complexities, facets, layers, and subtle (and not-so-subtle) variables and influencers related to trauma and its impact on today's student. No educator should be without this work in their personal and professional library.

William R. Keizer,
Frontline Professional Development

Introduction

The ideas I set forth are applicable in any adult learning environment, barring the sections that are specific to carceral[1] spaces. I have chosen to focus on incarcerated and formerly incarcerated learners, and the corrections environment, based on my experiences as an educator, academic, and student services professional. I have taught in free classrooms (i.e., non-carceral spaces), community spaces, and prison classrooms, with youth, young adults, older adults, and elders, and have used these principles in every setting.

Broadly, this book has three sections: 1) trauma and adult learning, 2) teaching in prisons and jails, and 3) repurposing education and learning. Any discussion or reflection on these topics must also examine organized education, systemic oppression, historical racism, power and relationships in the United States, the school-to-prison pipeline, and mass incarceration. Each of these related topics deserves detailed discussion, but this book does not give them that type of close attention.

The first section introduces different points of entry into trauma work, examines the connections between adult learning, trauma, education, racial and ethnic identities, and incarceration. The middle section examines teaching in carceral classrooms, a space where educators have minimal control over their environment, course content, and how much time they get with students. The last section looks at how we might change if we actively work to settle and expand the nervous system, tend our own pain and trauma, and embed joy into our teaching praxis.

This work is part of an emerging and expanding conversation about understanding trauma as it relates to adult education and learning. It has grown out of a multitude of vibrant, living, and long-running dialogues, and continues as part of the ever-growing discussion of how we teach and learn. This book fiercely challenges

1   our lack of understanding of the true impacts of trauma on learning,
2   the mythology that current educational systems serve all people equally,
3   narratives that some people who experience trauma are broken and in need of repair, while others are excused by the same narrative, and
4   a culture that has glorified one framework of knowledge and uses punitive educational systems to enforce that framework.

Teaching in carceral settings is a challenging task, and there is no in-depth professional training dedicated to preparing adult educators for its complexity and importance. Although I have used the population I am most familiar with, the ideas and concepts presented throughout the text can be shaped and adapted for most adult classrooms, learning spaces, and communities. In order to maintain the integrity of the work, any adaptation **must** be culturally specific and informed by the needs expressed by those most impacted.

DOI: 10.4324/9781003048312-101

It is critical that readers understand that although this book is about trauma-responsive education, *it is not a book about mental health, psychology, or social work*. I have deliberately avoided including information about specific fields of trauma work for this reason. Learning from this text will help you create a better personal service practice, but it will not turn you into a counselor, psychologist, or social worker. Do not make the mistake of believing that reading this book gives you any authority or license to speak with people about their histories and wounds, especially in carceral settings.

We all make mistakes. It is inevitable that you will hear stories, feel activated, or share without considering impact. I think back on my years of teaching, in and out of prison, and there are numerous moments I would handle differently now. Working with adults who have endured enormous trauma is challenging because we can inadvertently harm the people we are trying to help and, unlike children, adults are slow to forgive and trust again. Building relationships with adults is delicate work that can crumble in the blink of an eye.

Don't lose focus on your work and your role. You have an extraordinary opportunity to help people rediscover themselves as learners and their joy in learning.

Note

1 "of, relating to, or suggesting a jail or prison" (Merriam-Webster, n.d.), and expanding the definition to include transitional housing and juvenile facilities.

Chapter 1

Learning Our Context

As humans who are also educators, it is our responsibility to understand our context; how and where we are placed in our systems, groups, constellations, and relationships. These elements of who we are, and how we exist in the world also define who we are and what we bring into classrooms and learning spaces. This is not a new statement, but the call to understand ourselves more deeply has taken on a renewed urgency, driven in part by our collapsing climate, in part by increasing demands for systemic transformation and change around the world.

For those who work in institutions of higher education, the urgency is even stronger. Higher ed has long considered itself home to thought leaders and innovators possessing knowledge vital to our continued well-being. Higher ed has also been a bastion of Euro-White privilege, systemically denying access to BIPOC, disabled people, refugees, immigrants, and people living in poverty. This is changing, however, as the rise in communications and mobile technology make knowledge sharing less dependent on institutions of higher learning.

Colleges, designed to gatekeep and control access to information and upward mobility, find themselves floundering, unable to adapt swiftly enough to rapid waves of change. People who have been traditionally denied access and sent quietly on their way no longer are quiet, as long-silenced voices begin to loudly demand change. Lifelong academics, only now being required to examine their positionality, find themselves on uncertain footing, as cultural and academic norms shift and morph. The traditional roles of power and privilege no longer provide protection against systemic or individual examination.

We are complex beings, capable of holding complicated and opposing ideas. To believe that we are defined by only one aspect of ourselves is to deny our full capacity to learn, integrate, and grow. There are people who are grievously harmed by dominant culture and systems, and weaponizing context is a distraction, a way to avoid dealing with shame, guilt, and anger at either our own privilege or our own ignorance. It is both possible and imperative that we understand our places and roles in dominant systems in an effort to reduce harm to ourselves and others.

We all hold space in systems of oppression, and few of us exist in singular roles. Most of us have multiple, varied identities, and we may prioritize this or that one, depending on the circumstances of the moment. When I write about knowing our context, it is a call to see our gestalt; to lift ourselves from a background we may not recognize as our habitat.

Basic Concepts

There are certain concepts foundational to understanding the connections between trauma, mass incarceration, and corrections that are heavily referenced, but not deeply explored in this text. My recommendation is that you research these topics yourself, or use this book in

DOI: 10.4324/9781003048312-1

conjunction with learning about these other concepts. It is a lot of learning; much of it is going to take time to process and integrate into your practice. Give yourself plenty of space to reflect, talk with other people, and develop your thinking.

Dignity and Compassion

Treating people with dignity and compassion is non-negotiable in any trauma-responsive practice.

One of the hardest things to learn when working with people carrying high loads of trauma is what you can and cannot ask, and when it is appropriate to ask what. Even mental health professionals, if they are acting in a teaching capacity, need to consider their questions with great care. If you are a mental health practitioner, be cautious about where you engage in therapeutic work—public environments are not safe spaces for many people. Do not allow your curiosity to intrude upon another person's well-being.

A best practice for prioritizing relationships is to treat people as their innate humanity and dignity require—as worthwhile, deserving, fully complete beings who need offer no justification for who they are or their life circumstances.

Intersectionality

Trauma in education and prisons is racialized and intersectional. Hill Collins has written extensively about intersecting oppressions (Hill Collins, 2019), and Dr. Kimberlé Crenshaw (1989) coined the term "intersectionality" to explain how interlocking systems of oppression specifically harm Black women. Since its origination, the term has entered the mainstream conversation and Crenshaw, in a 2017 interview, noted that "Intersectionality is a lens through which you can see where power comes and collides, where it interlocks and intersects" (Columbia Law School).

Mass Incarceration

Mass incarceration disproportionately impacts BIPOC and disabled people and communities. It is the modern-day extension of Jim Crow laws and slave labor, further exacerbated by racist drug policies and militarized police forces across the United States. *The New Jim Crow* (Alexander, 2012) is one of the current definitive texts on the history and impacts of this extension of slavery and Jim Crow.

Organized Education

Organized education and learning are different, although there are overlaps. The phrase "organized education" includes all of our education-focused institutions, from kindergarten through post-doc, public and private schools and universities—any organization or institution whose primary purpose is to deliver education. These institutions have become cultural and economic gatekeepers, in part by diverting BIPOC and disabled children off the main pathways that provide access to economic mobility and, in too many cases, into the criminal legal system.

Educational systems and processes are designed from an exclusionary perspective, which means that for many, success is the exception, not the rule. Although it may try, organized education is not always a process for growth, development, and expansion, but rather a tool to bind the mind and spirit of those who do not or cannot fit into its rigid confines. For those who do not fit its narrow measure, success in such an environment requires extraordinary levels of compromise and compartmentalization, as well as sacrifice of the self. Even less often does this success result in true inclusion. In building such a rigid and exclusionary system, we have given ourselves no room for growth and expansion, no room to seek and integrate a balanced approach.

Despite this, I want to be clear that structured education is important. It is one way to transmit a shared understanding of the world and teach us how to think about, compare, and learn from common experiences. Like other major innovations, such as agriculture and science, organizing what we have learned and passing that learning on to our peers and next generations has been an enormous benefit for the human species. Without a transformative re-alignment, organized education will continue to perpetuate harm, falling far short of its potential as a life-affirming and creative endeavor.

School-to-Prison Pipeline

The school-to-prison pipeline starts impacting BIPOC and disabled children almost as soon as they start interacting with society. Foster care is a parallel pipeline, and organized education is a connector across the two. The NAACP Legal Defense and Educational Fund (2018) and the Marshall Project (2021) have both produced extensive, well-researched materials and recommendations.

Systemic Racism

Systemic racism exists and organized education is one of the structures that both protects and extends its survival. The Aspen Institute defines systemic racism as "A system in which public policies, institutional practices, cultural representations, and other norms work in various, often reinforcing ways to perpetuate racial group inequity" (2016). Dr. john a. powell prefers the term "structural racialization," noting that "[it] is a set of processes that may generate disparities or depress life outcomes without any racist actors. It is a web without a spider" (powell, 2013).

Terms and Phrases

This section defines or explains why I've chosen to use certain terms and phrases. Some are already in use; some are new or being used in a new context. With the rapid pace of linguistic shifts, it is likely these terms will need updating or additional conversation in the near future.

BIPOC

As defined by the BIPOC Project, the term BIPOC is used to "… to highlight the unique relationship to whiteness that Indigenous and Black (African Americans) people have, which shapes the experiences of and relationship to white supremacy for all people of color within a U.S. context" (2021). BIPOC is a term with its own complications, according to Jonathan Rosa and deandre miles-hercules, in a 2011 public discussion of the term "women of color" led by Loretta Ross. As acknowledged by these scholars, there is no "one size fits all" language or term when it comes to discussing race and ethnicity (Grady, 2020).

Ross notes, when reviewing the history of the term "women of color," that "[the term] has been flattened and lost its political meaning. Unfortunately, so many times people of color hear the term 'people of color' from other white people that they think white people created it," she said, "instead of understanding that we self-made it ourselves. This is a term that has a lot of power for us. But we've done a poor-ass job of communicating that history so that people understand that power."

miles-hercules notes that this is an ongoing struggle with language around race, especially as more and more white people enter the conversation. People are concerned about using correct language and not offending, but when any one particular term is adopted and used indiscriminately, it becomes problematic, and can, as Ross stated, begin to lose social meaning and power. Dichotomous Euro-white thinking also plays a role, as saying "Black is beautiful" (for example) is quickly interpreted as "white is ugly." Defusing this dynamic requires exhaustive effort, and results in less impactful language.

I have chosen BIPOC as it seems to be the most inclusive term, keeping the prior considerations in mind.

Cultural Rebalancing

This is not a new term, although it has been used mostly in contexts of economics and diplomacy. I use it in this work as a call to integrate and balance our approach to learning and education. I could have written under the blanket phrase "cultural competence," but "rebalance" is a more active term, and suggests that we act on the knowledge we gain.

It is not enough to know that other cultures exist.

Knowledge is a first step but without considered action, becomes a largely useless, theoretical endeavor. Putting knowledge into practice is not easy, especially knowledge that is outside of our familiar spaces. People who have only ever experienced (both in their childhood and adult education) one way of knowing may find changing their practice extremely uncomfortable, as they are asked to imagine not only experiences different than theirs, but worlds with different values, ways of relating, knowing, and understanding information.

It is not possible for members of the dominant culture to facilitate and lead while they are working to adjust and rebalance themselves. The work of cultural rebalancing must be led and facilitated by members of the de-prioritized culture. When done in this manner, the process itself becomes part of the rebalancing, and is both a means and an end. This presents problems, as BIPOC leaders are already exhausted and tapped out from surviving in racist systems, let alone teaching people how to deconstruct and transform those systems.

One solution to this seeming paradox is to pay BIPOC leaders well, provide hefty resources, and enforce accountability measures for anyone involved in this transformation. Educators should be on the leading edge of cultural rebalancing by looking to BIPOC to lead our efforts, integrating new knowledge into teaching practice, and bringing different ways of knowing and being into learning spaces.

Carceral Spaces

Most of my direct experience in corrections education has been with state prisons in Washington and Oregon, but state prisons are not the only places that offer educational programming for incarcerated people. Jails, federal and state prisons, and youth facilities (county, state, and community alternatives) are all carceral spaces.

Expansive Learning

The concept of expansive learning is covered in Chapter Six but is referenced earlier. Briefly, expansive learning is the opposite of, and has the potential to, counter the harm of educational trauma. It is a learning state that arises from being settled in the body (even if temporarily), stronger connections to higher learning centers, and activity that fosters expansion of the nervous system.

Incarcerated, Formerly Incarcerated, or System-Impacted Person

The Underground Scholars Initiative (USI) is the student organization that collaborates with the Berkley Underground Scholars (BUS). The organization is completely student run and the two bodies are aligned, but distinct. They "… define system-impacted as a person who is legally, economically, or familially affected in a negative way by the incarceration of a close relative. System-impacted also includes people who have been arrested and/or convicted without incarceration" (Berkeley Underground Scholars, 2019a).

Based on guidance from the USI in their 2019 "Language Guide for Communicating About Those Involved In The Carceral System" publication (Berkeley Underground Scholars, 2019b), I use these terms somewhat interchangeably. The USI publication provides definitions and guidance for a number of terms and, as with any group of people suffering under systems of oppression, taking guidance from them around language (and action) is required as we engage in this work.

Resilience and Empathy

"Resilience" and "grit" are a popular words right now, as researchers and practitioners both struggle to articulate why some people "succeed" and others "fail." I use the term and concept of resilience minimally because its cost is high and often born by the person or community that has been harmed. While resilience is a necessity for survival, praising people for resilience without aggressively working to dismantle oppressive structures is destructive and unacceptable.

Empathy is included in this section because it is also a widely used term that has a dark underbelly. Healthy, well-developed and -boundaried empathy can give us insight into how another person might feel, leading us to deeper understanding and, possibly, more compassionate responses. Dysfunctional empathy, however, can be a cover for unaddressed trauma and/or lead to incredibly destructive, toxic relationships and behaviors.

Although the concept of empathy is widely researched, instruction on how to develop high-functioning empathy is far less common. Healthy empathy, practiced with well-developed boundaries and not grounded in unresolved trauma is worthy of its own in-depth discussion and more than a passing mention in this text.

Settling and Expanding

In some fields of research, the word "settled" may indicate hypo-arousal, flat affect, or other "disassociated" state (Johnson, 2018), but I am choosing "settled" as used by Resmaa Menakem (2017). Merriam-Webster defines "settled" as (in part), "to cause to come to rest" and "free from distress or disturbance" (2021). "Expanding" is the process of creating room for our nervous systems to grow. These states are interdependent, and intrinsic to optimal conditions for learning.

Education as a trauma-responsive practice introduces settling and expanding as vital components of every adult classroom, especially when students may have high loads of unresolved trauma. In those spaces, teachers who are settled may see more responsivity and engagement from students, as their own nervous systems respond and begin to rest.

This calm, resting state is closely linked, if not identical to, the calm internal state necessary for learners to access their pre-frontal cortex, or higher learning centers. A settled state allows the body to relax and physically expand, which offers room for the nervous system also to expand. Given an ongoing restfulness, this settling and expansion may continue, transforming our state of being from agitated to settled, contracted to expanded, isolated to connected.

Some organizers and activists consider the language of "settling" problematic, including demands for emotional and self-regulation (Haines, 2019). Kai Cheng Thom notes that a "return to safety" may not be possible for oppressed people, and that self-regulation "implies the control and domination of mind over emotion & sensation[1]." Both of these perspectives reinforce our need for broadening our approach to trauma.

Trauma-Responsive

Mainstream conversations about trauma-informed care, education, treatment, and so on have grown rapidly in the last few years, although our language has remained fixed in the idea of healing as a goal, an accomplishment, something to be attained. We are better served when we consider "healing" as every aspect of a journey to wholeness; re-finding the fullness of ourselves in relationship to self, community, nature, and spirit. This movement, from healing as a point on a line to redefining the line itself, begins with developing more nuanced language to address the continuum of trauma work.

The term "Trauma-Informed" was coined by Maxine Harris and Roger Fallot (2001) and, according to the Buffalo Center for Social Research, "Trauma-Informed Care understands and considers the pervasive nature of trauma and promotes environments of healing and recovery rather than practices and services that may inadvertently re-traumatize" (The Institute on Trauma and Trauma-Informed Care (ITTIC), 2021).

This is a descriptive, comprehensive definition for those working for systems change, especially health professionals, and harm reductionists. Over the last several years, the phrase "trauma informed" has become an umbrella term, expanding to cover an enormous body of research and practice, both individual and systemic. Even as more and more people and organizations look to apply a trauma-informed approach, the gap between knowledge and application, especially for non-mental health professionals, widens. We hear enormous bureaucracies claim to implement trauma-informed approaches, when it is clear that their practices are continuing to harm and retraumatize.

The spectrum of traumatic experience is vast and we do not have a widely accepted or easily accessible method to measure or describe the impacts of non-physical trauma (i.e., emotional, mental, spiritual). Even a discussion of "measuring" trauma is problematic, as it defaults to Euro-white demands for quantification, turning trauma and healing into objects, parts of a whole that must be measured and catalogued. While there is value in certain aspects of this approach, it is incomplete and unbalanced.

I chose the phrase "trauma responsive" because it requires activity and engagement, not just knowledge. That activity and engagement can be determined by the practitioner, but must come from a place of care, integration, and cultural balance.

The Language of Healing

Almost any conversation about trauma includes the concept of healing. Who doesn't want healing, for themselves or others? What we miss in the quest for "being healed" is that healing is a process, not a stopping point. "Heal" is a word like "love," "pain," or "hate." It is impossibly general, even as it can be applied to any number of specific examples. In all my years as an educator, I never considered myself a healer, or thought of my students as people who needed healing. Most educators I know have said the same, many are adamant that the language of healing not enter the classroom.

I agree, not because I think learning is not healing, but because what we think of as "healing" may or may not be what happens in learning spaces. This is a serious deficiency in both our language and our thinking about the nature and presence of trauma—especially trauma that is unseen but not unfelt. Many types of trauma extend far beyond the physical, into the realm of the heart, intellect, and psyche, hindering our ability to interact with other people, communities, spirit, our planet, and care for ourselves. For these unseen wounds, the metaphor of physical healing extends only so far.

Different modalities (e.g., movement, land-centered practice, art and creation, spirit-focused, community-centered) require that we choose, or create, new language, and that we broaden and deepen our understanding of the phrase "trauma work." At best, the language of healing is ambiguous in the context of educational practice. The concept of healing—who needs it, who doesn't, who is the healer and who is the healed—is complex and, in this particular context, ill-defined.

Across many conversations with other colleagues in practice, we agreed that removing the language of "healing trauma" serves two purposes.

1. Decenters the instructor as the (benefactor or bestower) of healing.
2. Removes the assumption that certain groups require healing (i.e., they're broken) while others (including educators themselves) are able to ignore or bypass the necessity for doing their own healing work.

Educators, and others, need a way to think about and approach working with trauma that is appropriate to the spaces they create and inhabit. Classrooms and other adult learning spaces are often public, with little or no privacy, institutional (i.e., square, interior facing, fluorescent lights, uncomfortable seating, rows, stale air and odors), and people in them are strangers, with individual goals and limited time to build relationships or understanding. These constraints act against our current definition of healing, in almost every context, even though we know that learning spaces can be places of growth and expansion.

As I work through my own traumatic experience, I use different language, as illustrated in Figure 1.1.

I created this illustration to share my process, and demonstrate the importance of new language. I can access each stage separately, spend whatever amount of time I need, and move on to something else—a different stage or topic. For every topic I uncover that requires attention and care, I accept it as part of my life's work. Menakem and van der Kolk (2014) both discuss recognizing and releasing trauma to make more room in the body and nervous system. Sometimes the word "healing" is appropriate, but more often I use "integrate" to describe how my understanding has fit itself into my body, psyche, and place in the world.

I use the word "healing" occasionally but generally try to avoid direct mentions of what happens in trauma process work. Trauma-responsive education does not require or even recommend that we determine what is happening in a learner's heart, mind, or body at any given moment. If you do choose to use this language, I encourage you to begin with your own work. Practice noticing and learning how each phase feels. Any work around trauma can easily lead to more harm, so take great care and caution when you bring new concepts into your actual praxis.

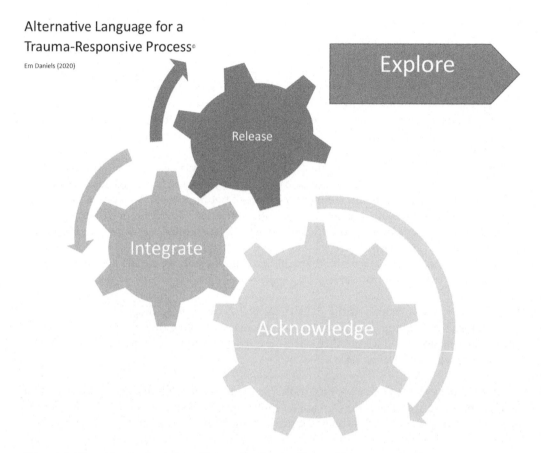

Alternative Language for a
Trauma-Responsive Process©

Em Daniels (2020)

Figure 1.1 Alternative Language for a Trauma-Responsive Process©.
Source: Daniels, M (2020), Spokane WA. Copyright (2020) by M. Daniels. Reprinted with permission.

Urgent Considerations

I am writing this book, in part, to explore questions emerging from the intersection of education, learning, trauma, and corrections. Some are new, but most are long-standing and even more urgent in the face of sweeping movements for social justice and change. Lacking an actual number, I speculate that ~95% of research about incarceration and its long-term impacts is done on, by, and about Euro-white men. Even though Black, Indigenous, and Brown men are disproportionately represented in every level of the criminal legal system, the research is done from a Euro-white perspective, through a Euro-white lens, with Euro-white goals and outcomes. Also of note is that the topic of disability is largely invisible in almost every aspect of the mass incarceration conversation, despite high numbers of incarcerated people with diagnosed and undiagnosed disabilities.

Missing Genders

Although men, by far, are incarcerated in greater numbers than women, women have been the fastest-growing demographic for the last two decades, increasing more than 700% from the 1980 to 2019, where over 60% of women in state-run prisons are mothers of minor children (The Sentencing Project, 2020). According to prisonpolicy.org, "Incarcerated women are 53% White, 29% Black, 14% Hispanic, 2.5% American Indian and Alaskan Native, 0.9% Asian, and 0.4% Native Hawaiian and Pacific Islander" (Kajstura, 2019).

We have little data on intersectionality specifically with regard to women, but close to 30% of women in prison identify as lesbian or bisexual. From what data we do have, it is clear that Black, lesbian, and transgender women are at greater risk of arrest and longer sentences, whether in jails or prison. Many of these incarcerated women are the primary caregivers for their families, and their families suffer the consequences of imprisonment with them. According to NICIC, "5 million children—7% of all US children—have had a parent in prison or jail at some point" (National Institute of Corrections, 2019). Parental incarceration, especially for poor families, is devastating and many never recover economically or as a family unit.

The field of gender, learning, and education is extensive and has a rich history that, to this point, includes minimal (but growing) scholarship on women in prison[2]. More current scholarship includes examining the intersections of women, race, ability, sexual orientation in the carceral environment as a newer field, and it needs more voices.

Box 1.1   The binary designation

For more information on the rights of incarcerated trans people, please see Lambda Legal and National Center for TRANSGENDER EQUALITY (2019).

There is some advocacy and understanding of the impacts of incarcerating mothers, and women generally, but it is not enough to counter the glaring lack of justice-focused, actionable research about the impacts of incarcerating women on families, especially the impacts on communities of color.

Willful Ignorance

There is a wealth of scholarship from Black thinkers, activists, and academics on mass incarceration and its impact, and while that is not the focus of this text, it is impossible to discuss any aspect of the prison industrial complex, the school-to-prison pipeline, and all of its attendant cottage industries without discussing race. As many in the United States grapple with their complicity in mass incarceration as an extension of Jim Crow, we find ourselves squarely in front of an institution that starkly illustrates an ongoing crime against humanity; a result of our inability to address historic, systemic racism.

Even though race is a primary element of prison culture, there is no understanding or acknowledgment at any level of the corrections hierarchy, of historical racial trauma or systemic oppression that I have witnessed. It is hard for me to imagine that our current system could change enough to include such understanding, nor do I believe it desires such a change. The discussion about reallocating police funding to community organizations, public health, and social safety nets MUST expand to include all of law enforcement, not just the police.

The Trauma Umbrella

Research on trauma and education is still largely under the umbrella of children and early childhood development. Exploration of trauma and adult learning is so new that it is hard to know if there are notable, actionable differences across the range of gender identities, race and ethnicity, or sexuality. There are certainly differences in approach based on age and the developmental spectrum, but research and practice focus primarily on early childhood.

Experience tells me there are observable differences across the range of intersectional identities that include race, ethnicity, gender, and ability. It is unclear how external circumstances such as socioeconomic status and intergenerational access to education impact these intersections, although it is hard to imagine they do not. These are all deficiencies in our understanding, but we are only at the earliest beginnings of our explorations. This is a hopeful moment, as how and what we research and investigate are not fully determined. We have a wide horizon of opportunity to shape and guide decisions about how and what to explore.

Other areas with little or no easily accessible writing, research, or advocacy (that I could find):

• Culturally appropriate research in almost any aspect of corrections including education and learning, "rehabilitation," mental health, and ability/disability;
• De-institutionalization and returning to the community;
• Implementing trauma-informed policy and practice in an environment where trusting relationships are often not possible; and
• Critical examination of our current measures of success and obsession with "data-driven" and "evidence-based" approaches as elements of Euro-white values and perspectives, excluding other measures, approaches, and definitions of success.

On the Sidelines

Why has higher education been absent from these conversations for the last 20 years?

The field of education and its academics pride themselves on being at the cutting edge of learning, knowledge, and thinking but with few exceptions, has largely ignored both the field of corrections education and the needs of currently and formerly incarcerated people altogether. This should not be a surprise, given the inter-connectedness of mass incarceration, racism, and organized education, but it is past time for this complicity with oppressive systems to end. Dr. D–L Stewart's challenge to higher education to rethink its foundation and purpose (Stewart, 2020) could easily be brought to bear in the context of corrections education and support for reentry.

Community colleges are the workhorses of corrections education, but they have rarely brought the topic of corrections education and the students they serve to broader higher education conversations. While corrections education departments function almost as entire colleges on their own, the nature of working in a prison usually results in a peculiar isolation from regular campus activity and culture. Unless the department makes constant efforts to stay connected, it is largely invisible, which means the knowledge and experience of those staff and faculty remains untapped.

Higher education in prison conversations are often focused on increasing the presence of four-year universities and liberal arts education in prison settings. While making education accessible to more people is critical, these conversations can overlook the work already being done by community colleges, community-based organizations, and volunteers. These conversations may also focus on content, minimizing discussion of the need professional development for faculty, comprehensive, ongoing training and support for all staff who work inside, and how best to serve students upon their return to the community.

Colleges could be building pathways from prison to the free campus, educating faculty and staff on issues facing reentering students, making efforts to include the voices of incarcerated students in student life and government, and actively taking steps to dismantle discriminatory educational practices but this opportunity has been almost entirely ignored. Even worse, colleges and universities will often discriminate against these students as they attempt to transition to free campuses upon release, or refuse to hire people based on their conviction history.

Questions we should be asking include

- Why are there states that do not offer education while people are incarcerated?
- What are best practices to help ensure consistent, compassionate education while people are incarcerated?
- How can our colleges and other educational institutions best support people who are returning to their communities?
- What can schools and colleges on the outside do to support and work with schools and colleges on the inside?
- How do we better support staff and faculty who work in one of the most stressful and toxic environments imaginable?
- How can we better support corrections professionals who may not have had access to education?

The Rise of Online and Remote Learning

As COVID-19 shut down most schools (K–12 and beyond) across the country and the world, the rise of online learning was rapid and steep. Lack of access to mobile technology (laptops and tablets), software, and infrastructure (i.e., high speed internet) bleakly highlighted long-existing equity gaps. Students who had relied on access through campuses, libraries, and other public spaces were suddenly cut off even as schools scrambled to move as much as possible online. Students who would never have chosen to attend online found they had no option if they wanted to continue their education, complete programs, or receive financial aid.

Nowhere did this overnight shift to online learning have a more devastating impact than in carceral spaces. What education programming was available disappeared, as carceral institutions simply stopped allowing educators inside, or to communicate with students via instructional packets or standard postal service. Although facilities have been considering introducing secure Internet, almost none have, so face-to-face instruction has been the only option for most corrections education departments. The long-standing belief that face-to-face education is the only modality of value has resulted in programs rejecting correspondence and remote learning.

While facilities in some states have focused on finding technology that will meet multiple purposes, the process is slow at best and ground almost to a halt during the first year of the pandemic. For several months, the only way educators and staff had to stay connected to students was via correspondence and that can be hit or miss, depending on institution policy and practice.

What I have learned from leading scholars and activists in the field of higher education in prisons is that privileging face-to-face education, personal interactions prioritizes

- One cultural approach.
- Certain types of communication and interaction.
- Synchronous communication.
- A specific type of educational experience (usually what we had).
- A particular type of community and/or interpersonal relationships.
- Real-time content development and sharing.

While we all have personal preferences, we cannot ignore any modality that has the potential to keep students and scholars engaged and certain that we value them and their scholarship.

Setting Limits

Making decisions about what to include in a topic that touches so many areas was (and continues to be) a daunting prospect. I consistently asked myself, "Does this directly impact adult learning, or adult learners in carceral spaces?" and if the answer was not clearly "yes," then I set that topic aside. I decided also that since I am not a scientist or mental health professional, I needed to maintain a layperson's perspective on trauma, as much as possible.

I found it a bigger challenge to limit my critique of the criminal legal system and corrections in particular. My original drafts were much more critical of these systems, but I chose a more neutral approach for three reasons:

> First, an abundance of scholars, activists, and organizers have been writing about and working for change for decades. They have produced extensive scholarship, wisdom, and direction for transformative, systems change, and it is a topic that deserves more than a passing mention or two in this book.

> Second, it is my hope that this text will be used by teachers and scholars in many different fields, including corrections. With this in mind, especially in Chapter 4, I attempted to report my observations with as little opinion as I could manage. Sometimes naming and describing a thing is all that is needed to make a point or raise a question.

> Third, mass incarceration—specifically prisons and jails—harms everyone, including the people who work in those institutions. True justice, true transformation, and restoration require inclusivity and accountability, and there is no easy starting point for these conversations.

I am not an expert in working with victims and crime survivors, and have not included that perspective in this work. I support the right of victims of crime and their families to pursue healing and resolution in the ways best suited to them, and in their right to be heard in a much more inclusive way than they often are now. It is also important to note that many system-impacted persons are victims and survivors even as they are convicted and incarcerated as perpetrators of crime.

My first instinct in writing is to use a feminist/womanist lens, but I made a deliberate choice to de-centralize that perspective. In part, I made this choice because the language and field of feminism, womanism, and gender (broadly) is rapidly shifting and growing and is outside my current field of research. But my primary motivation is that mass incarceration has been a racialized issue since slave catchers became law enforcers, and it continues as a racialized issue. It is difficult to find culturally balanced information on incarceration, and even less is available addressing gender.

Lastly, I did not include any stories or details from my classrooms that would violate our classroom confidentiality agreements.

Notes

1 I was unable to confirm where this was originally published, although I did reach out to the author: https://www.facebook.com/133041234078/posts/kai-cheng-thom-writes-i-think-the-major-difference-between-a-social-justice-and-/10158089327834079/
2 Stephanie Covington is one of the foremost experts on the intersection of gender, trauma, addiction/recovery, and corrections. She is a renowned researcher, practitioner, and author of the widely acclaimed text Beyond Trauma: A Healing Journey for Women (2nd Edition), and its accompanying curriculum. She can be found online at https://stephaniecovington.com/.

References

Alexander, M. (2012). *The new Jim Crow*. New York, NY: The New Press.

Berkeley Underground Scholars. (2019a). *Our mission*. Retrieved from https://undergroundscholars.berkeley.edu/about

Berkeley Underground Scholars. (2019b). *Underground scholars language guide: A guide for communicating about people in the carceral system*. Retrieved from https://undergroundscholars.berkeley.edu/blog/2019/3/6/language-guide-for-communicating-about-those-involved-in-the-carceral-system

Columbia Law School. (2017). *Kimberlé crenshaw on intersectionality, more than two decades later*. Retrieved from https://www.law.columbia.edu/news/archive/kimberle-crenshaw-intersectionality-more-two-decades-later

Crenshaw, K. (1989). Demarginalizing the intersection of race and sex: A black feminist critique of anti-discrimination doctrine, feminist theory and antiracist politics. *University of Chicago Legal Forum, 1989*, 1 (Article 8) 139–167.

Grady, C. (2020). *Why the term "BIPOC" is so complicated, explained by linguists*. Retrieved from https://www.vox.com/2020/6/30/21300294/bipoc-what-does-it-mean-critical-race-linguistics-jonathan-rosa-deandra-miles-hercules.

Haines, S. K. (2019). *The politics of trauma: Somatics, healing, and social justice*. Berkley, CA: North Atlantic Books.

Harris, M., Fallot, R. D. (2001). *Using trauma theory to design service systems: New directions for mental health services*. San Francisco, CA: Jossey-Bass.

Hill Collins, P. (2019). *Intersectionality as critical social theory*. Durham, NC: Duke University Press.

Johnson, R. (2018). Trauma and learning: Impacts and strategies for adult classroom success. *MinneTESOL, 34*(2), 1–9. Retrieved from http://minnetesoljournal.org/journal-archive/mtj-2018-2/trauma-and-learning-impacts-and-strategies-for-adult-classroom-success/

Kajstura, A. (2019). *Women's mass incarceration: The whole pie 2019*. Retrieved from https://www.prisonpolicy.org/reports/pie2019women.html

Lambda Legal. (n.d.). *Transgender incarcerated people in crisis*. Retrieved from https://www.lambdalegal.org/know-your-rights/article/trans-incarcerated-people

Menakem, R. (2017). *My grandmother's hands*. Las Vegas, NV: Central Recovery Press.

NAACP LEGAL DEFENSE AND EDUCATIONAL FUND, INC. (2018). *Dismantling the school to prison pipeline*. Retrieved from https://www.naacpldf.org/wp-content/uploads/Dismantling_the_School_to_Prison_Pipeline__Criminal-Justice__.pdf

National Center for TRANSGENDER EQUALITY. (2021). *Police, jails & prisons*. Retrieved from https://transequality.org/issues/police-jails-prisons

National Institute of Corrections. (2021). *Children of incarcerated parents*. Retrieved from https://nicic.gov/children-of-incarcerated-parents

powell, j. a. (2013). Deepening our understanding of structural marginalization. *Poverty & Race, 22*(5), 3,4,13. Retrieved from https://www.prrac.org/pdf/SeptOct2013PRRAC_powell.pdf

The BIPOC Project. (2021). *About us*. Retrieved from https://www.thebipocproject.org/about-us

Settled. (2021). Retrieved from https://www.merriam-webster.com/thesaurus/settled

The Aspen Institute. (2016). *11 Terms You Should Know to Better Understand Structural Racism.* Retrieved from https://www.aspeninstitute.org/blog-posts/structural-racism-definition/

Stewart, D. -L. (2020). Twisted at the roots: The intransigence of inequality in U.S. higher education. *Change: The Magazine of Higher Learning, 52*(2), 13–16. doi:10.1080/00091383.2020.1732753

The Institute on Trauma and Trauma-Informed Care (ITTIC). (2021). *What is trauma-informed care?* Retrieved from http://socialwork.buffalo.edu/social-research/institutes-centers/institute-on-trauma-and-trauma-informed-care/what-is-trauma-informed-care.html

The Marshall Project. (2021). *School-to-prison pipeline: A curated collection of links.* Retrieved from https://www.themarshallproject.org/records/67-school-to-prison-pipeline

The Sentencing Project. (2020). *Incarcerated women and girls.* Retrieved from https://www.sentencingproject.org/publications/incarcerated-women-and-girls/

van der Kolk, B. (2014). *The body keeps the score.* New York, NY: Penguin Books.

Chapter 2

Learning Is the Human Condition

People want to learn. The desire to learn, and grow based on that learning, is fundamental our human experience. It is the call of the soul and it drives us as much as the need for physical survival. Freire speaks of humans as "unfinished" and "that [our] unfinished character... and the transformational character of reality necessitate that education be an ongoing activity" Freire (1972, p. 84). Knowing how to learn is one of the most valuable skills any person can develop and it is impacted, guided, and directed by an almost infinite number of variables. Once we grasp how fundamental learning is to human existence, the importance of our ability to and capacity for both learning and integration increases dramatically.

Learning is full of complexity, and to say that there is only one right way to learn and know the world is to limit the fullness of our experience. Every aspect of our experience teaches us how to adapt and survive, thrive and explore, relate to others. Our circumstances and environment teach us how we are perceived, and how those perceptions influence our relationships with others. We learn what it means to be a certain type of person, what knowledge is important, how to make meaning of events, and how to integrate all this information into ourselves, our families, and communities.

Observing and relating to others is one of the most immediate ways we define what it means to be human. Developmentally, babies and children are dependent on the people around them to learn how to use their bodies and senses, get their needs met, and begin communicating and relating.

Our patterns of relating and communicating, of understanding how to best get our needs met, are formed at such an early age that we are barely conscious of their presence. The same is true of how we process and prioritize information. The "how" of our knowing is programmed into us from our time in the womb, and we are rarely, if ever, asked to consider that our "how" is not the only "how."

How we learn and how we relate are two of the invisible elements of teaching. We may question the content we are tasked with delivering, but not the structures that define our teaching models, physical environments, the influence of wealth, evaluation and assessment of success, or even the purpose of organized education in the United States. We have accepted a particular "how we know" and that "how" influences every aspect, every nook and cranny of our lives.

Power and knowledge have always been entangled, and our current model of education clearly illustrates this entangling. The "how we know" is inseparable from how we relate to each other and the role of power in those relationships. Adults physically dominate children, limit knowledge, control physical space and how children can move their bodies, and are the ultimate executor of punishment or reward. Punishment and reward are based on a host of invisible criteria (that many teachers may not even realize they are using) as well as correct consumption of content. Children

DOI: 10.4324/9781003048312-2

who do not meet these criteria are punished, with the implication that a mistake is somehow a moral failure.

I did not enter teaching thinking about any of these issues; about oppression and struggle, moral failure, power structures, or the nature of how I know and relate to others. When I began my quest to become a better teacher, I could not articulate what "better teacher" meant or why it felt so important. I didn't have the words or concepts to describe what I was seeking, I knew only that we were missing something, some way of knowing or being that could make us better teachers.

Seeking this undefined element has taken me from one end of a spectrum to another; from education as content delivery, subordination, and indoctrination, to learning for growth and evolution. Our learning cannot continue to come only from fear and desperation, it must grow and evolve if we are to grow and evolve. We must expand beyond the boundaries we have created, learning and teaching from that expansion; evolving not from destruction but creation.

In the United States, organized education is how we codify specific types of learning and relating and those lessons permeate our culture far beyond any classroom. The system does serve other purposes for a particular demographic of students, although they also would benefit from a flexible, expansive approach to education. Our current system

1. Reflects a paradigm grounded in domination and subjugation that prioritizes Euro-White ways of knowing and understanding the world.
2. Is tasked with indoctrinating students (of any age) into that paradigm.
3. Suppresses and punishes those who resist this educational indoctrination.

None of these purposes serve us individually, as a nation, or as citizens of the world. They do nothing but keep us firmly in the grip of survival and fear-based thinking and living, unable and unwilling to access our full potential as creative beings. Using education in this manner also prevents us from taking the revolutionary step of resolving our own trauma instead of systemically inflicting it on others.

Unresolved trauma and shame are the glue that holds our destructive frameworks in place. Mass incarceration is, perhaps, the most clear and direct manifestation of the path we have chosen—a path of pain and humiliation, forged in domination, white supremacy, bound in place by unresolved trauma, rage, and shame. That education plays a primary role in perpetuating these systems of fear and domination is a tragedy of unspeakable magnitude.

Our personal work, as educators, is to deeply feel that tragedy and not shrink back in shame, or turn away in disgust or self-loathing. We cannot do this if we have not acknowledged, resolved, and integrated our own pain. Because unresolved trauma is the binding agent, the most radical, transformative work is on ourselves. As long as the binding agent remains the same, we will perpetuate the foundation and shape of these structures of harm.

As we transform ourselves, the reflective shape of those systems must also change. When we are connected to each other through joy and creative endeavor, our systems and processes will reflect these life-affirming attitudes. As it is now, our world wavers on the cusp of destructive choices, our unaddressed collective and individual pain laid bare.

As we move into a discussion of how we know and relate, it is important to stay connected to our overall purpose and not get lost in comfortable daydreams, or a cloud of intellectualization. Each of these directly contributes to educational trauma and mass incarceration, the measurable suffering of BIPOC and disabled people and their families, and to ongoing systemic racism and dehumanization. Teasing out how these components are entangled is the first step in understanding the potential far-ranging impacts of a trauma-responsive teaching practice.

How We Know

We are all intuitive, although the degree varies, and we can choose to develop our intuitive nature, or not, as we please. We talk about intuition with respect to almost every aspect of human life and endeavors, especially in terms of making choices and taking risks. It is terribly easy to conflate intuition with learning and, as we use what we have learned, can become terribly difficult to disentangle the two. As we integrate what we learn, we begin to believe that we have always known it, that things have always been this way, and we forget that we ever *didn't* know.

While most educators do have an innate teaching sense, that sensitivity is developed as we connect and integrate knowledge through hundreds of hours of experience and reflection. Good teachers don't just happen; they are the result of incredible dedication and care, often at great personal expense. Being a good educator is hard and oftentimes painful work. We are keenly aware that our mistakes not only impact us, but can have long-standing negative impacts on our students.

We are interdependent and our work should reflect and highlight that interdependence. The spark of the idea might be mine, but the kindling was already laid and the flames belong to everyone. Without reminding ourselves who came before us, on whose shoulders we stand and on whose land we walk, we turn the corner into believing that this or that idea originated with us. Without these reminders, we lose the lineage of ideas, imagination, vision, joy, pain, and scholarship that brought us to this point, and that loss should be unbearable.

Writing this chapter challenged me to

1. articulate why I think what I think and feel what I feel. Saying "it just *felt* right," or "it was my intuition" was not only unhelpful to readers and practitioners, it negated my efforts to develop a thoughtful, considered approach to my practice.
2. differentiate my original ideas from those of my intellectual ancestors and influences. Scholars, activists, mystics, theorists, educators, practitioners, friends, mentors, and colleagues whose words and thoughts and feelings I had shared over the years—all have contributed to my personal and professional development.

As part of this process of articulation, I drew heavily on the work of bell hooks (1994, 2001), Raine Eisler (Eisler and Miller, 2004), and Patricia Hill Collins (1990). I am using Jones and Nichols' work on epistemology "to provide a careful comparison of how different ethnic groups approach knowledge, and how that influences our being in the world" (2013). hooks, Eisler, and Hill Collins all speak extensively about power, race, and gender.

Though organized education is only a percentage of our learning journey, it exerts an extraordinary amount of influence through shaping **how** we learn and how we think of ourselves as learners. It also has defined "successful" education and the ensuing rewards for success and punishments for failure. While the field of education expends considerable effort in examining aspects of learning and effectiveness, it has long denied its role as an oppressive power and cultural suppressor.

Philosophies of Knowing

Our differences do not inherently create conflict, but conflict arises from that aspect of human nature unable to cope with beings who approach and enter the world in different ways. Much of our education (formal, informal, cultural, societal) is about delineating these differences, the history of violence and atrocity committed in the name of those differences, and endless examples of the problem itself, with few solutions presented. If HOW we know and engage with the world has created so many of the problems we face, then that same HOW will not also present solutions.

Societies and cultures have developed unique ways of learning and integrating knowledge but in the United States, the Euro-white framework of standardization and quantification, as defined by Jones and Nichols has become the dominant paradigm. In the table "Philosophical Aspects of Cultural Difference Connecting the Past to the Present to the Future" (2013, p. 37), they present a detailed comparison of how "ethnic groups who came to the US and groups who share an ethnic worldview" approach knowledge and knowing.

> Euro-white/Euro-American peoples know the world through counting, measuring, object acquisition, induction, linear, and binary thinking, as well as looking to quantify and replicate behavior and outcomes.

> African-American/Latinx/Arab and Middle Eastern peoples know the world through personal relationship, imagery, rhythm, and storytelling; big-picture thinking; going directly to the core of the problem; and joining of opposites.

> Asian/Asian-American/Polynesian peoples most value group cohesiveness, striving for transcendence, cycles and repetition, viewing all aspects simultaneously, and a world that exists outside of ourselves.

> Native American peoples experience the world through melding with spirit, knowing through reflection and openness of spirit, cycles as showing the whole, and environmentally experiential reflection.

As we look at this portion of their work, it is apparent that US institutions such as law, education, culture, economics, and healthcare have systemically centered Euro-white approaches from the moment of their creation. While other frameworks gain notice from time to time from within the confines of the Euro-white system, they are not accepted as fully functional and desirable on their own. People and organizations that attempt to center other ways of knowing find themselves forced to integrate Euro-white approaches, or be excluded and cut off from needed resources.

How does this impact our systems of education and why does it matter?

Inside a framework that has dominated our thinking for hundreds of years, recognizing individual examples against its all-encompassing background can prove a challenge, but a closer look at higher education demonstrates that it is firmly cemented in the Euro-white framework. Higher education glorifies quantification, standardization, acquisition, and measurement, and rewards scholars and institutions who prioritize these aspects of learning. We see this in our obsession with data and evidence, demands for ever more rigorous grading, prizing intellectual development at the expense of the emotional, natural, and spiritual self, which careers and industries are incentivized, and types of research receive recognition and donor dollars.

The connection between wealth and quality of education is well-documented in both scholarly and popular writing. If a family has wealth, they live in districts with good schools and can afford supplemental instruction and activities. Their children are accepted into colleges that offer a stunning combination of learning experience, cultural immersion, and relationship-building that all but guarantees intergenerational wealth growth (the foremost measure of success in the United States). Not surprisingly, these families operate within the Euro-white framework, and these children are well-suited to succeed in educational systems that privilege their ways of knowing and interacting with the world.

Families without significant wealth, which includes many BIPOC families, do not have the same relationship with education. While education is seen as a pathway to a better future, access to that pathway is fraught with systemic and individual racism and oppression, lack of access to resources, and the burdens of historic trauma. Because the impact of mass incarceration on Black, Brown, Indigenous, and poor families has been so extensive, we also cannot discount the impact of intergenerational incarceration on those families, or the lack of intergenerational access to education.

This is not to say that the Euro-white approach is inherently wrong, it has expanded our understanding of our world and the universe, leading to improvements in quality of life and health. But while this approach is useful, the extreme imbalance in prioritizing its requirements above all others is unsustainable and destructive. As we examine learning from a trauma-responsive perspective, those who have experience only with the Euro-white model must deliberately seek, engage with, and integrate multiple knowledge frameworks. This process will change how you understand and interact with the world and this is what we need in order to thrive as a species.

How We Relate

Relationships with other people are necessary to our health and well-being, although those relationships can also be primary causes of our individual traumatic experiences. In the United States, our relationships are primarily based on a "power over," or Dominator, model. In this model, power is limited, must be hoarded, and is wielded to ensure compliance and obedience.

This model is replicated in almost every relationship we experience or observe throughout our lives—one person (or group, organization, company, etc.) has power and they wield it, like a weapon, to ensure their needs, or wants or desires, are met. They may also wield their power and authority as a way to create safety for themselves, feel powerful, avoid discomfort, maintain advantage, hoard resources, or gatekeep access to knowledge.

These dynamics are alive and well in our families, adult/child relationships, friendships, workplaces, faith institutions, schools and colleges, entertainment and games, romances and marriage, communities, natural resources, and all the endless ways humans relate to themselves and the world. Mass incarceration and the resulting carceral spaces are a peak expression of this "power over" dynamic in modern US history.

Law enforcement agencies, founded as slave-catching entities, embody this dynamic on the streets, and again in prisons and jails. Once a person's physical body is placed into confinement, their will to consent legally removed, they are entirely at the whim of the people who control their body and environment—hidden from accountability and oversight by the smoke and mirrors of public safety.

hooks (1994, 2001), Hill Collins (1990), and Eisler and Miller (2004) all speak to this terminal (as in "leads to death") power dynamic in far greater depth and nuance. Eisler writes more generally to the "power over" dynamic of the Dominator model. hooks and Hill Collins speak, respectively, to the "politic of domination" and "Matrix of Domination" with a Black, feminist approach that is directly relevant as we discuss mass incarceration. All speak about education and its role in perpetuating relational power dynamics, both implicitly and explicitly, on individual, systemic, and cultural levels.

The Role of Power

Power is the invisible member of every relationship. Whether it is a relationship between people, objects, systems, or our environment, its presence is never questioned and rarely discussed. Much of our maneuvering in relationships is to determine who controls the power, positioning **ourselves** to hold power, take advantage of the person who does, or avoid their wrath. People are rarely comfortable discussing power dynamics because, in many cultures, you are either the dominator or the dominated.

People with power don't want to talk about how they use that power because that could lead to accountability, or others trying to wrest power from them. People without don't want to talk about power because they want to avoid being the subject of its abuse. People respond to such challenges in different ways, but those in positions of unexamined power, especially power conferred by position, are apt to retaliate. We all learned early, from our teachers and other powerful adults, that challenge, even unintended, equals danger and retaliation.

This—the unchecked retaliation of teachers and other positionally powerful adults—is a key part of our assimilation into the systems that continue to harm us.

Eisler, Freire, Hill Collins, and hooks all note that the role of education is indoctrinate children (and adult refugees and immigrants) into the hierarchies and matrices of domination (race, gender, ability, and class) that subjugate their lives in the United States. Perry (2006) and Menakem (2017), in discussing responses to trauma, both acknowledge that people subjected to constant pain and oppression find ways to not only numb their own pain, but to suppress empathy and inflict their pain on others.

Organized education is, in part, the outcome of merging:

1. Unacknowledged, unresolved pain, and its avoidance responses.
2. Euro-white philosophy that centers objectification and possession, assessment and replication, and siloed, decontextualized knowledge, and
3. Dominator relationships.

Those of us who traveled the path of organized education were (and are) taught to internalize the unchecked Dominator power model, look to others to define our worth and value, and accept those decisions, and normalize receiving punishment for not learning or behaving according to a set of unspoken, invisible rules deemed the "correct way." For prison educators, this means you will have an abundance of students whose self-image as learners is badly damaged or non-existent.

We have created and live in a society based on and dedicated to domination, but this is changing, even as that change is agonizingly slow. Over the course of my career as an adult educator, I have witnessed a shift in our collective mindset and the backlash such shifts inevitably attract. I am not surprised that the resistance and backlash to even the appearance of change is extravagant and violent. Across the world and throughout history, people, systems, governments, and institutions have rarely given up power willingly and the United States is no different.

How We Teach

How we teach is the culmination of how we know and how we relate. It is where the rubber meets the road, where we place ourselves into practice. If we have not cultivated an approach to teaching that is different than what we experienced as children, our best intentions are little better than wishful notions. It is inevitable that we will replicate our own educational experience. It takes courage, commitment, and fortitude to overcome our own indoctrination and training in both the Euro-white knowledgescape and Dominator relationships.

We must understand these pieces of our context. Our context defines who we are and what we bring into classrooms and learning spaces and the call to understand ourselves more deeply has taken on a renewed urgency. For those who work in institutions of higher education, the urgency is even stronger. These institutions are cultural and social mobility gatekeepers, having long defined one of the major pathways to success the United States and until we address this legacy of control and exclusion, we cannot create a new future.

Our context includes placement in systems of oppression, but few of us exist in singular roles. Most of us have multiple, varied identities, and we may prioritize this or that one, depending on the circumstances of the moment. When I write about knowing our context, it is a call to separate ourselves from our gestalt; to lift ourselves from a background we may not recognize as separate from ourselves. It is both possible and imperative that we understand our role in the dominant system, even as we may have suffered harm from that system or others.

We are complex beings, capable of holding complicated and opposing ideas. To believe that we are defined by only one aspect of ourselves is to deny our full capacity to learn, integrate, and grow. There are people who are grievously harmed by dominant culture and systems, and weaponizing context is a distraction, a way to avoid dealing with shame, guilt, and anger at either our own privilege or our own ignorance.

Even if we have the necessary elements and interest, we cannot begin to de-program ourselves without understanding the various pieces in the systems that have shaped our knowing and thinking. There are three elements in the "how" of teaching that drew my interest.

1. The language we use to define the act of teaching, i.e., "pedagogy" and "andragogy."
2. Acknowledgment, articulation, and critique of the banking model of education.
3. Stewart's writing on the fundamentally racist roots of higher education (2020).

Pedagogy and Andragogy

I was originally not going to discuss pedagogy or andragogy but changed my mind after much conversation with other adult educators, especially those working in carceral settings. The "how" of teaching is where oppressive, abusive systems manifest abusive, racist, misogynistic policies and practices. This happens along the entire spectrum of teaching: children, young and older adults, public and private schools, corporate training, religious institutions, military academies, prisons and jails, and it happens in and across these institutions, not just in classrooms.

I had long used "pedagogy" as a catch-all term to describe my teaching approach and style. While definitions of both pedagogy and andragogy refer to teaching methods and styles, inherent in andragogy is that "andros- (or man)" is the default for all people, while pedagogy derives from "paidos" which means "boy, child."

Both words, at their roots, accept the male as the default setting for all people, although our collective understanding has changed over time. Continuing to use words rooted in exclusion is not my preference but they are the words we have at the moment.

Trauma-responsive practice requires an intentionality that includes choices around language. Adults are not children and you cannot use the same practices and approaches with adult learners as with children, especially when it comes to trauma. Teaching adults is different than teaching children, and exploring that difference reveals our thinking that children must be controlled, but adults must be allowed some freedom of self. The connection between educational trauma and punishing a child's autonomy are strong, and should highlight the urgency of changing our approach to teaching children.

Box 2.1 Further discussion of pedagogy and andragogy

As noted by Mercanti (2015, p. 3), when discussing cultural transformation, a more accurate word than patriarchy is androcracy, "...from the Greek root words andros (man) and kratos (ruled), to describe a social system ruled by men."

If we look at the word "andragogy," we see the similarities: Andragogy is made up of the Greek roots *andr-* ("man") and *-agōgos*, ("leader"), making it literally mean "leader of man." The first record of andragogy in English comes from the 1920s, but it is based on a German term, *Andragogik*, that was introduced by German educator Alexander Kapp in 1833 (Andragogy, n.d.) and (Andragogy, n.d.).

The word "pedagogy" is similarly biased: "Pedagogy is another word for education, the profession and science of teaching. Pedagogy and pedagogue come from the Greek paidos "boy, child" plus agogos "leader." Pedagogy refers to the teaching profession as well as the science of education, for example as a college subject" (Pedagogy, 2021).

I know there are schools and individual educators who treat children as people: capable, intelligent, and worthy of being treated with dignity. Systemically, this treatment is not assured or consistent, especially for BIPOC, poor, and disabled students. The surge in online teaching and learning has, maybe more than any other event could have, highlighted massive disparities—lack of Internet access, technology, and, as technology was developed on Euro-white cultural models, the increased difficulty for some students in simply attempting to navigate the demands of online learning.

When we teach children, our focus is on their development. They take in everything—what we teach, how we teach, things spoken and unspoken, social cues, and so on. People love to teach children for many reasons, and teachers have enormous influence over how children develop as learners, especially their degree of confidence in themselves as able to learn, integrate, and grow. When children are unable or unwilling to force themselves into the stereotype of a "good student" as defined by our current systems, that system takes steps to either force them to fit, or discard them.

The first steps happen in the classroom, where adults play a dual role—teacher and punisher. As we have seen, students who do not fit the "standard" expectations of teachers, are often subjected to an escalated need for control in Dominator power relationships. As these students struggle to understand an entire suite of invisible expectations that include class, gender, and race-based communication, learning styles, and cultural references and norms, they are also attempting to learn whatever content is being disseminated.

At this point, conformity is conflated with content consumption so if a student cannot or will not conform, they are assumed to be incapable of learning the content. Their struggles with and resistance to having to change themselves (in deeply troubling and profound ways) simply to learn are warranted. Teachers who may not have resisted (or needed to resist) Dominator education, do not understand what is happening. When the adult authority is unable to force the student to conform, the conflict is escalated again, to the next level of Dominator relationships—parents, principals, and, ultimately, law enforcement.

Pedagogy, by definition, reinforces the "power over" dynamic, where andragogy at least acknowledges autonomy and the desire for self-actualization (even if its root ignores the presence of women and non-binary people). While focusing solely on the individual remains problematic, it has its uses and can be a doorway to other work, especially in deconstructing toxic power dynamics both in community and one to one. As educators, we have the potential to be at the forefront of this change, whether we work with children or adults.

Though the focus of my work has been adults, I have strong objections to even this basic definition of pedagogy. Teaching children to depend on others for knowledge and evaluation, without also teaching autonomy, equality, interdependence, and the importance of personal experience perpetuates the cycles of socio-emotional violence and Dominator culture that pervade our society. Perhaps this definition is not indicative of the field of K–12 teachers, as individuals, but systemically, it is what we have built.

Children and adults require different teaching approaches but it is clear that most people who find themselves teaching adults have only their own learning experiences as a point of reference. I use the word "find" with deliberation. The number of people who are trained in adult education and then go on to actually teach adults is small. The number of people who end up teaching adults because they have content expertise is much larger. We have created a system that relegates teaching to a throwaway profession; a contempt exemplified by the phrase "if you can't do, teach."

Adults carry their childhood experiences and trauma, often unacknowledged and unresolved, and this presents a complex challenge when unacknowledged, unresolved childhood educational trauma reveals itself in the classroom. When this happens, teachers often revert to treating adult students like children—a strategy based in misunderstanding the difference between pedagogy and andragogy. It is important not to treat adult students, no matter their educational experience, as lacking intelligence, capacity for learning, or as dependent solely on content experts for all knowledge.

Teachers are conditioned to think content alone addresses the needs of adult learners—a direct replication of the "content expert" pedagogical approach. Teachers replicate their experience as students, during their K–12 years and on through higher education. When a teacher has never experienced an equitable classroom, where their voice and experiences were highly valued, they are unable to replicate that experience for their own students.

While working with children is seen as an opportunity to avoid inflicting harm, I rarely hear adult educators discuss this topic. That is unfortunate, as adult learning spaces can be quite harmful, inflicting new trauma and reinforcing prior damage. Any discussion of andragogy should include, at the least, the topic of harm reduction.

Banking Method Education

The banking method of education, as defined by Freire (1972) and further examined by hooks (1994) is a well-defined example of how Euro-white knowledge structures have dominated both what and how we know. In this model, education is a collection of products for consumption by objects (students) and teachers (Subjects) are the experts. They make deposits into the students, knowledge is not co-created, lived experience is not valued or acknowledged, and students are given voice only to repeat what they have been fed.

As Subjects, teachers are given individual authority over students' experience, in both what and how they should learn. This authority demands not only that the object consume knowledge, but that it consume, relate, and reflect that knowledge in the correct way. Combined with the Euro-white framework, knowledge itself is separated from context and lived experience. Information—data—is viewed as wholly objective, able to exist independently of consumers, observers, or users. In this way, the banking approach simultaneously upholds the Dominator relational model and centers Euro-white ways of knowing. As many teachers themselves were objects in banking education, they are familiar enough with how it operates to step smoothly from object to Subject.

Despite attempts to democratize learning, any person who participated in organized education has experienced being the object in the banking model dynamic. I grew up in a military family and attended several K–12 schools. In the quest for my graduate and undergraduate degrees, I attended five community colleges, three universities, and took many community and corporate training courses. I have worked at a university and two community colleges, as well as an alternative high school, as a corporate trainer, and community educator.

During my time in all of these spaces, as object and Subject, I encountered a range of teaching styles, the majority clustered near the banking end of the spectrum. Even in large, liberal universities, banking style education dominates. Subjects with content expertise (a white, male majority) are handed extraordinary individual power over the learning experience, shoring up the banking system and Dominator model. Teachers at all levels are incentivized to protect their expertise and authority and, by extension, to gatekeep academia more broadly.

More than once, I experienced public anger from teachers who felt that even a mild questioning of dogmatic ideology or incomplete perspective was too much. At that time, I struggled to understand what I had said or done that had engendered such an aggressive reaction, and I often internalized the narrative that it was somehow my fault. In my own time as the Subject, I also have reacted poorly to questions and challenges, responding to these natural learning attempts as if they were challenges to my personal authority and expertise.

Now, having been an educator for over two decades, it is clear that teachers (myself included) who overreact in this manner are committed to the illusion of themselves as experts. They are the Subject and the object role is to listen and absorb, not question. The Subject and object have, at best, minimal relationship beyond dispensation, consumption (including judgment of that consumption) of neatly quantified and packaged artifacts in a transactional exchange of "knowledge."

Perhaps of more urgency, the banking model has vilified ways of knowing that it perceives as different. Students who require rhythm, movement, vocalization, ritual, orientation toward nature, different learning tools (screen readers, audio-content) and a focus on relationship are not only overlooked, in the K–12 system they are actively and aggressively punished. This punishment, for Black, Indigenous, and Brown children (especially boys) and disabled students often results in suspension, expulsion, and early contact with law enforcement. We punish these children because they seek knowledge and learn in ways that teachers have been taught to view as threats to their authority.

This mindset encompasses our entire system, from kindergarten to the highest degree levels, and it makes sense that people who have been disallowed to fully participate in their own learning would then turn around and inflict that same disallowance onto their students. Without someone to call their attention to the cycle, and help them break it for themselves, it is hard to see how they would teach differently than they were taught.

Even with all the harm it does, the system does offer a series of rewards for those who are able to assimilate, or seem to assimilate, enough to pass its tests and gain passage to its inner workings—the hallowed halls of academia.

The Gentleman Scholar

We find the "Gentleman Scholar" seated firmly at the intersections of Euro-white philo-sophies of knowing, banking method education, and Dominator models of relationship. As Stewart (2020) notes, specific behaviors, values, and ways of knowing are consistently re-warded, while others are systemically excluded or punished. Attempts at equity fail because the markers of "success," as well as the requirements to access the Ivory Tower of academia, firmly center Whiteness, maleness, and other models of domination.

When an entire system is designed to vigorously protect access to power, any change requires far more than simple understanding. Education in prisons is not designed for lib-eration or "rehabilitation," it is designed to produce workers (via vocational training), re-plicate itself through creating more "Gentleman Scholars," or reinforce toxic power hierarchies by forcing students to subjugate themselves to content experts for validation. A trauma-responsive educational practice, on the other hand, both strengthens the ability to learn, and educates for liberation and expansion.

Having a solid grasp of our most common relational dynamic, the Dominator model that Freire's Subject/object dynamic illustrates, opens a door to practice new relational models. If we examine our relationships, especially in the classroom, we see that organized educational spaces are critical in conditioning us to accept domination with regard to learning, and in society. As we work to liberate ourselves from this dynamic, we can seek to create space to normalize power sharing.

A new dynamic also recenters the learner as the voice of their own lived experience and sole decider of its worth. This is not merely reformation, this is revolution. Discarding the need for external validation as we accept our internal power places us in a position to observe and interact with compassion and understanding, and decline to engage with toxic power struggles.

Addressing power dynamics in the teaching/learning space is a vital trust-building element that we must not overlook. Beginning a conversation with students (and others in the room) about how to build and maintain relationships, address conflict, give and receive feedback, and take responsibility is a first step co-creating a power-with environment. Equitable learning spaces give us and our students a place to experience our relationship to power differently.

Where We Are

Every moment we are in learning spaces is a moment of reckoning. These moments happen for us individually and collectively—small groups, institutions, collectives, community or-ganizations, government, nationally, and globally. We have the choice, in every moment, to face and reckon with our past, or continue in the darkness and shame of denial. Reckonings are hard. Reckonings come along because we were unable to face and accept our suffering, and the suffering we have caused. Educators, at all levels, must accept responsibility for what education has been and done, systemically, as we accept our own individual positionality in systems of oppression.

Delaying accountability only increases its necessity, and our fear at being held accountable makes us weaker, crueler, and smaller. We will not survive as a species if we cannot reckon with and learn from our history, then use that integrated knowledge to move into our better selves.

References

Andragogy. (n.d.). Retrieved from https://etymologeek.com/eng/andragogy

Andragogy. (n.d.). Retrieved from https://www.dictionary.com/browse/andragogy

Eisler, R., & Miller, R. (2004). *Educating for a culture of peace*. Portsmouth, NH: Heinemann.

Freire, P. (1972). *Pedagogy of the oppressed*. New York: Herder and Herder.

Hill Collins, P. (1990). *Black feminist thought: Knowledge, consciousness, and the politics of empowerment*. New York: Routledge.

hooks, b. (1994). *Teaching to transgress: Education as the practice of freedom*. New York, NY: Routledge.

hooks, b. (2001). *All about love*. New York, NY: Harper Collins.

Jones, B., Nichols, E. (2013). *Cultural competence in America's schools*. Charlotte, NC: Information Age Publishing.

Mercanti, S. (2015). Glossary for cultural transformation: The language of partnership and domination. *Interdisciplinary Journal of Partnership Studies, 1*(1), 1–35. doi:10.24926/ijps.v1i1.89

Pedagogy. (2021). Retrieved from https://www.vocabulary.com/dictionary/pedagogy.

Perry B. D. (2006). Fear and learning: Trauma-related factors in the adult education process. *New Directions for Adults and Continuing Education, 110*, 21–27.

Porter, L. (2016). *Dear sister outsider*. Retrieved from https://www.poetryfoundation.org/articles/89445/dear-sister-outsider

Stewart, D. -L. (2020). Twisted at the roots: The intransigence of inequality in U.S. higher education. *Change: The Magazine of Higher Learning, 52*(2), 13–16. doi:10.1080/00091383.2020.1732753

Chapter 3

Learning and Trauma

Trauma shapes the human experience but, as Menakem reminds us, it is not destiny. From birth, through every step of our lives, we are exposed to suffering through circumstances and events, our own decisions, as a result of structural and historical harm. Humanity has evolved by surviving trauma, so we have no true, conscious insight into how a non-traumatized brain might look, act, or feel. It is not unreasonable to ask if we should consider normalizing trauma—if we should begin with the assumption that every person has current, past, or historical trauma present in their lives. Pain is a common thread, tying us to others' experience.

Alternatively, fear of that pain forms a wall that isolates us, in an attempt to protect our tender hearts. This refusal to acknowledge our own suffering is a second thread of commonality. We expend tremendous amounts of energy denying our pain, and hiding from the pain of others. This reservoir of unacknowledged, unresolved pain holds our broken systems in place, even as we witness ongoing cycles of oppression and death. When we face this truth, we can admit that healing our own wounds, tending our own suffering, and refusing to pass our pain on to others, is a necessity.

As we learn, we can make different choices, choices rooted in connection and care. Instead of binding ourselves with unacknowledged, unresolved pain, we can actively imagine and work for connections grown from shared accountability and a desire for growth; connections that hold without binding and encourage us to explore with flexibility and curiosity. We can integrate different ways of experiencing the world, building a way forward that celebrates this glorious coming-together. We can learn to be fuller expressions of ourselves as humans.

Intersecting Assumptions

We begin with the knowledge that society is built on a variety of interlocked systems that prioritize

- Euro-white (predominantly male) ways of knowing and thinking;
- relating through domination;
- cultural assimilation via organized education; and
- expertise based on rigidly controlled knowledge consumption.

Freire introduced the concept of *conscientization*, "The process of developing a critical awareness of one's social reality through reflection and action" (p. 44). If learning happens in ways specific to our different frameworks, but our system of education recognizes and allows only one way, then we have no conscientization about the learning process and what constitutes strong learners in other frameworks.

DOI: 10.4324/9781003048312-3

Much, if not all, of the science of learning focuses on what is needed to be successful in the Euro-white knowledgescape. Within that framework, the research focuses heavily on cognition, and the importance of well-developed cognition as intrinsic to any learning process. From this perspective, "compromised learning" means that cognitive functions are underdeveloped, weak, or not easily accessed. Other aspects of our learning selves are either not considered or given no true importance. Although we have some knowledge on how to counteract impacts of trauma on cognition, we are far from a full understanding of how to best help strengthen learning that is grounded in other ways of knowing.

Cultural competency is a requirement for a trauma-responsive practice. While you may not be an expert in a certain type of cultural practice, you can acknowledge its importance and welcome it into the classroom space. Understanding that students may experience safety and belonging in different ways is a necessary step in building an environment and practice that honors and seeks a variety of cultural expression, with a focus on expansive learning. This does **not** mean that the traits we do know about are unimportant in other frameworks, or on their own merits. It is likely that certain traits hold value across groups, but it is as likely that there are traits being overlooked and ignored.

Theoretically, we can try to separate the presence and impacts of trauma from societal structures, but in reality they are impossible to untangle, just as we cannot separate our physical bodies from our emotional and intellectual selves. Organized education is an integral societal structure that models the only example of teaching that most of us ever experience. Without developing a critical awareness of the systems we inhabit, we unconsciously continue cycles of harm.

But this does not have to be our destiny. We can rebel against **how** we were taught and teach others differently. In this rebellion, trauma-responsive practice has the potential to become a form of liberatory education.

Assembling the Pieces

When I began researching trauma, incarceration, learning, and adult education, I was stunned that so much of what I had done to help students reflected the principles of Trauma-Informed Care. Trauma-Informed Care is heavily informed by research in the fields of sexual assault and domestic violence, but includes work from activists, organizers, and experts in community health and well-being. The work is often led by mental and social health experts, and has grown to include recommendations and best practices for systems-level change.

The two elements that drew my attention were:

1. Shifting our queries from "what's wrong with you?" to "what happened to you?" (Bloom, 2007).
2. Implementing a Connect, Protect, Respect, and Redirect approach (Hummer, Crosland, & Dollard (2010).

People working on the front line of helping professions, teaching, disaster response, and other fields have long known that trauma was a "thing." They may not have known the science behind it, but they certainly knew that when someone came in with physical signs of assault, that they needed to be cared for in certain ways, would react better to certain types of questions and body language, and might need specific types of care. To this point, we have all been using similar approaches, most centered in mental and physical health, combined with some level of harm mitigation.

But trauma has a much bigger umbrella, even though the individual fields of research and practice have stayed somewhat separate from each other. Raphael, Wilson, Meldrum, Bedosky, & Sigman (2000) define trauma using eight general dimensions:

- "Threat to life or limb;
- Severe physical harm or injury, including sexual assault;
- Receipt of intentional harm or injury;
- Exposure to the grotesque;
- Violent, sudden loss of a loved one;
- Witnessing or learning of violence to a loved one;
- Learning of exposure to a noxious agent; and
- Causing the death or severe harm to another"

I include these because they are widely accepted and relevant, but I find them incomplete and culturally imbalanced. I have assembled the following collection of categories and experiences to address those gaps:

- "Single incident trauma is related to an unexpected and overwhelming event.
- Complex or repetitive trauma is related to ongoing abuse.
- Developmental trauma results from early exposure to ongoing or repetitive trauma.
- Historical trauma or (Inter-generational trauma) is a cumulative emotional and psychological wounding over the lifespan and across generations emanating from massive group trauma.
- Intra-generational trauma describes the psychological or emotional effects that can be experienced by people who live with trauma survivors" (Walker, 2014).
- Systemic trauma is the ways that our social arrangements—governments, economies, religions, etc.—put individuals and populations in harm's way (Galtung, 1969).
- "Adult onset trauma happens after the childhood developmental stages and has a different set of impacts on both identity and psyche, and
- Massive (group) psychic trauma concerns how small or larger numbers of people are impacted by events such as war, climate disaster, intra-state/governmental violence, and so on" (Boulanger, 2011).

The drawback of lists like this is that they are overwhelming, and offer no clear starting point for people unfamiliar with students' trauma histories. Even with that information, how would we use it in a classroom setting? How would we best help the person sitting in front of us after such revelations? How do we help ourselves if our own unresolved pain is activated? None of these questions is particularly useful in the context of adult education but, until now, educators have had few alternatives.

I imagine that most people, like myself, either avoided personal topics completely, graded upsetting assignments, or struggled through many awkward, ill-advised conversations. Nor surprisingly, the research suggests we refrain from questions and, instead create a practice that broadly addresses the impacts of trauma on learning. Regardless of their history, educational practice can be structured to help students prepare for learning without delving into their traumatic experiences.

Disrupted Development

Trauma disrupts brain development and operation. Developmental impacts happen during childhood, operational impacts can happen across the lifespan. These disruptions can change how we learn, and what we can understand and integrate. Even if the trauma is not physical in nature, the physical structures of the brain, the networks and pathways and connections, may be changed in ways that can never return to a fully pristine state.

My starting assumptions are that

1. a healthy survival mechanism/response is critical;
2. accessing the higher centers of learning is a positive and necessary action for us to move beyond baseline survival;
3. in order to move beyond just survival, we have to build wider pathways and stronger connections between survival centers and executive functions;
4. people who live in a constant low-level state of fear and stress are unable to consistently and strongly access their higher center of learning; and
5. there may be other centers of learning impacted by trauma and unknown to me.

Trauma inhibits development in children, and can also result in a wide range of poor long-term mental and physical health outcomes including heart disease, frequent mental distress, obesity, and diabetes (Burke-Harris, 2019; CDC, 2021; Gray, 2019; Menakem, 2017; van der Kolk, 2014; Zelenz, 2020). With regard to brain development, specifically, it can turn developmental progression upside down (Ohio Department of Education, n.d., Weinhold, 2015), and change the brain's capacity to both acquire new and retrieve stored information (Perry, 2006). When adult learners return to the classroom, they bring the cumulative burden of personal trauma, systemic oppression, and the learning impacts of educational trauma. This accumulation of stress and fear destroys the capacity for learning.

Common behavioral impacts include: impaired memory, lower verbal skills, increased acting out **and** internalizing (depression, anxiety, withdrawal), lower test scores, short attention span or easily distracted, difficulty with self-regulation, more discipline referrals and suspensions, and inability to maintain healthy relationships with other children. Perry (2003) describes the threat response as existing on a continuum, moving from a state of attentive calm through arousal, into alarm, and ultimately ending at fear.

In a *calm* state, ability to learn is unhampered by stress-related cortisol in the brain, and people are able to access their pre-frontal cortex, the seat of "higher" thought and learning. The body relaxes, and is not preparing for a physical threat response. They can engage their memory, critical thinking, and perception, focusing on words and verbal communication. This is the state necessary for collaboration and high levels of creative problem solving, so the closer students move toward the state of attentive calm, the more able they will be to access the areas of the brain needed for learning.

Gray, Perry, and Zelenz tell us that when people are *aroused*, they focus on the concrete—what is immediately in front of them, tasks they need to accomplish, and what they need to remember. Most people spend the bulk of their educational experience in a state of arousal, and organized education reinforces these behaviors through domination and control. The state of *alarm* tips us into our emotionally reactive selves. Our bodies and minds constrict, becoming rigid and inflexible, and we are unable to concentrate on anything beyond the immediate environment.

Once we enter the *fear* state, learning is relegated entirely to the survival system. We detach and may struggle to recognize the people and environment around us. None of our higher functions are available to us, nor can we respond to others' attempts to soothe us using reason and logic. Frightened people are in a constant state of low-level arousal. They are too busy scanning the environment for potential threats to concentrate on future planning, making meaning and interpreting texts, connecting with fellow students and teachers, or pondering abstract concepts.

Adult students who enter the classroom with significant childhood or educational trauma likely enter further toward the fear end of the spectrum, in a low-level threat response from the first moment. Even if these students have found ways to cope with childhood trauma, if this is their first venture back into education, that educational trauma may be close to the surface and extremely sensitized. For BIPOC students, culturally relevant trauma work is imperative in order to not continually re-harm and re-traumatize (Narine, 2016).

Our bodies are not built to maintain this constant state of threat arousal but in traumatized people, the body is unable to regulate its stress response back to a normal state. This dysregulation leads to increased and persistent levels of stress hormones which keep the body in a constant state of physical threat arousal. One consequence of the overlong presence of these chemicals is disruption in neural and cognitive development, which leads to specific difficulties with learning. Instead of the brain integrating and balancing its survival and cognition centers, the focus remains on survival and information not directly relevant to survival may go un-integrated.

This information, stored while the learner is in a fearful state, either must be retrieved from a similar state, or the retrieval itself throws the learner back into the fear state. Learners raised in persistent-threat environments are rarely able to obtain (even with artificial means) the internal state of calm necessary to higher learning (Perry, 2006) and (Schiffmann, 2017). Trying to store data while in the fear state is like trying to save a document while a computer is crashing. The computer might save pieces of data, but they cannot be retrieved as a coherent whole, nor is there an integrated context.

Perry and Boulanger (2011) both note that dissociation is a common response, especially when physical responses (fight, flight, fawn, freeze) are not available. This is probably the most common response I saw in my prison classrooms, as people had little recourse to any type of overt physical or emotional response. In the dissociative response, students withdraw—the blinds go down—and they turn their attention inward. Most of us have had experience either teaching or sitting in a classroom with someone who has dissociated. Even if we don't interact with them directly, it is easy to spot someone who has "spaced out," or daydreams constantly.

Attempting to re-engage students who have withdrawn can be a challenge. Traditional approaches are likely to escalate the fear response and result in increased shutdown or strengthened defenses. Casting back to what van der Kolk tells us about the rational brain attempting to engage the emotional brain, it seems that an intellectual attempt to re-engage a dissociated person would encounter a seemingly irrational resistance. With our new understanding, however, that dissociation seems more likely an *emotionally* rational attempt to deal with a perceived threat.

Because learning is hard-wired into being human, a perceived lack of interest in learning should no longer be considered an issue of motivation. It's not that people aren't motivated to learn, but that other things are physiologically or chemically rendering learning inaccessible beyond basic survival and immediate concerns. For prison educators, this is especially true. People living in prison are in constant-threat environments. Even the most dedicated and persistent students are, on some level, always managing the effects of living in a threat-heavy environment.

Inherited Pain

We are learning that trauma is passed down genetically, which means that historical trauma also plays a role in how people learn to thrive or not. Children of survivors of genocide (e.g., Native and Indigenous peoples, Holocaust survivors, Cambodians, Rwandans, and enslaved Africans) may be at significant and severe disadvantages in much of their learning, from birth onward. Not only have many of these peoples suffered systemic and structural brutality and oppression, their unhealed and unresolved trauma may be shared across generations.

The Centers for Disease Control (CDC) define epigenetics as " ... the study of how your behaviors and environment can cause changes that affect the way your genes work. Unlike genetic changes, epigenetic changes are reversible and do not change your DNA sequence, but they can change how your body reads a DNA sequence" (What is Epigenetics?, n.d.). One area of study in the rapidly expanding field of epigenetics is concerned with how trauma changes both how DNA is read and how those changes become intergenerational. Children inherit not only their family culture, they may also inherit the trauma and responses, as passed through that culture into their DNA. Scholars and scientists in the field of epigenetics are working to increase our understanding of historical trauma, its transmission, and current manifestations.

While our species has evolved through trauma-based learning and we all have that history encoded in our DNA, suffering is not distributed equally. Certain groups are more subject to historical and structural harm than others, but trauma has impacted how all of us have evolved. Responses to trauma, especially to group traumas, such as slavery or genocide, can be passed from generation to generation. Individual coping strategies can be seen as defects, even as they are internalized and start to look like culture. This is called traumatic retention, and may also be known as a "soul wound," especially in the context of Indigenous culture and healing (Duran, 2019; Menakem, 2017).

Intergenerational cycles of pain and abuse are not new. It is well-established that people are pre-disposed to treating others the way they have been treated, especially when we look at abuse and domestic violence. We watch as friends, loved ones, clients, and even ourselves, repeat old relationship patterns, even if we know those patterns are harmful. It should not surprise us that those experiences change us on a basic physical level, and that we can pass those changes on to our children.

Recent scholarship has demonstrated that BIPOC as children suffer significantly higher levels of stress during childhood and adolescence, resulting in higher accumulations of stress hormones, and dysfunctional cortisol levels, both linked to fatigue, depression, impaired memory and cognition, and a range of poor long-term health outcomes (Deardorff, 2015; Levy, Heissel, Richeson, & Adam, 2016).

These children also suffer the cumulative impacts of structural and institutional racism and discrimination which leads to poor health outcomes as well as fewer educational and socio-economic opportunities, and an increased risk of interaction with the criminal legal system. In their K–12 years, BIPOC are more likely to be suspended or expelled and less likely to be noted as gifted or exceptional within the school system (Nittle, 2018).

The negative impacts of systemic and structural racism on educational attainment and success cannot be overstated. The combination of daily stress, historical trauma, structural inequity, and negative educational experiences all combine to create an environment that is anything but conducive to learning and healthy development. When we match this research with the demographics of mass incarceration, it is clear that as adult students walk into prison classrooms, many will have this deeply embedded physical and emotional memory of their educational experience.

Trauma Goes Mainstream

Trauma became a topic of mainstream conversation after Kaiser and the CDC published their joint findings in 1998 in the Adverse Childhood Experiences (ACEs) study (Centers for Disease Control and Prevention, 2021). The ACEs has been of enormous benefit, providing an access point to begin understanding the science behind traumatic experience. According to the Kaiser website "The study, released in 1998, was one of the largest investigations of its kind and illuminated the connection between childhood trauma, stress, and maltreatment with health and well-being later in life" (Kaiser Permanente, 2019). One of the study findings is that the US population, as a whole, averages an ACE score between 1 and 3, leading to the conclusion that we are all subject to some type of trauma as children.

The revelation that there are serious, long-term health consequences of emotional, mental, and physical abuse has dominated mainstream conversation in the last 10–15 years. Even within this conversation, we underestimate the both the weight of traumatic experience and its lingering pervasiveness. Reviewing the demographics and responses in the study, it is abundantly clear that the ACEs represented only a thin slice of the population. It was also clear that that slice did not include the majority of my students—poor, BIPOC, with disabilities, and inheritors of legacies of intergenerational pain.

The foundation of the study itself—a partnership with Kaiser insurance and the CDC—calls to mind participants employed by businesses that could afford to offer Kaiser insurance in the 1980s and 1990s, not people living at or below the poverty line as most incarcerated people. Study demographics show 74.8% white, 4.5% Black, 11.2% Hispanic, 7.2% Asian/Pacific Islander, and 2.3% Other (Centers for Disease Control and Prevention, 2021). These numbers roughly align with population percentages in the country overall, although the percentage of Black study participants is very low by both today's numbers and the mid 1990s.

Reviewing the study through my experience working in prison and reentry, I thought the scores were probably much higher, at least for the people I worked with. I since have discovered I am not alone in my thinking. According to Weinhold, "…clinical research indicates that many people either forget these ACEs, or create stories to 'normalize' them. This means that the extent of these effects is understated. In addition, our experiences with helping people uncover their hidden developmental traumas showed that many of developmental traumas are caused by neglect. [Neglect as an ACE]… was not researched in these studies and is even more difficult to remember" (2015).

I wondered if having knowledge of an ACE score would inform my teaching, or change students' learning. Initially, it seemed safe to assume that people with significant childhood trauma would have more intense and, perhaps, more pervasive learning challenges. It also seemed reasonable to assume that people who had a smaller amount of trauma might have less challenges with learning.

I wanted to find out more, but I am profoundly grateful that I did not pursue that line of thinking. I cannot imagine a non-harmful outcome of a teacher asking a class full of students about their childhood traumas in an attempt to piece together a new teaching approach. No matter how well-intentioned the teacher, every outcome of that scenario is bad for both students and teacher. As I researched, I found far more questions than answers: How exactly are we measuring trauma? Beyond poor health outcomes, what are we discussing? How do we consider intergenerational and systemic trauma? How do we understand progress, both individually and collectively? What do we truly need to know to best help people?

It is possible we will never have answers, or that we will only develop answers as we rebalance ourselves culturally, and abolish mass incarceration. It is possible we simply aren't evolved enough yet to understand what we are asking about, let alone be able to measure, describe, or define it in a specific way. Menakem and others note that trauma is not destiny, but I believe that what is not destiny is **unending** suffering. Pain is a necessary part of life, as shadow is a necessary part of light, and destruction a necessary part of creation. I feel and see and hear our work as drawing in to each other, inhaling and exhaling together, using trauma and integration to find our most complete selves.

Entering the Work

When Bill and I began presenting on incarceration and adult learning, we quickly realized that the true heart of our discussion existed in the intersection of trauma, education, and incarceration. We spent our first year working together trying to find ways to talk about our ideas that weren't focused on mental health, prison culture, or violence prevention. We were both uncomfortable with education framed as healing, and educators as healers, and we went to great lengths to emphasize that what we were teaching did not give people freedom to act as counselors or social workers.

We struggled to adapt this approach and language, understanding that we had to use the tools available, although they did not accurately express the nature of our work. Beyond accuracy, we immediately understood that attempting to frame teaching as a healing practice presented practical problems:

- Educators do not consciously equate education with healing.
- Classrooms are not healing spaces for everyone. For BIPOC and disabled students, there is often painful history associated with education and this is especially true for prison classrooms.
- There has been minimal crossover from the field of trauma-informed research and practice into the larger field of adult education. Even the most committed teachers have had few easily accessible resources that did not have the potential to do more harm.

When I began writing, it became obvious that I would have to resolve this issue. I needed to write about education and teaching as trauma responsive, while removing the expectation of healing embedded in the research and language. My experience and research all pointed to the idea that if trauma itself is such a complex, multi-layered entity, our efforts to learn about and understand its role in our lives must also be complex and multi-layered. The metaphor of physical healing is simply not robust enough, and does not fully capture the range of traumatic experience.

To address this shortcoming, I created Figure 3.1 to illustrate eight approaches to working with traumatic experience. These approaches already exist, although not all of them have been considered specifically in terms of handling trauma.

Our massive cultural imbalance has limited our thinking about trauma in ways that come into sharp focus when we discuss learning. By centering cognition as the primary indicator of ability to learn, we have forced ourselves into examining the impacts of trauma only on cognition in relationship to learning. But I know that while cognition is one part of learning, there are other ways of knowing and experiencing the world that do not consider it the only or even primary method for learning. This topic alone is deserving of an entire field of research but for now, we will use the following definitions as starting points:

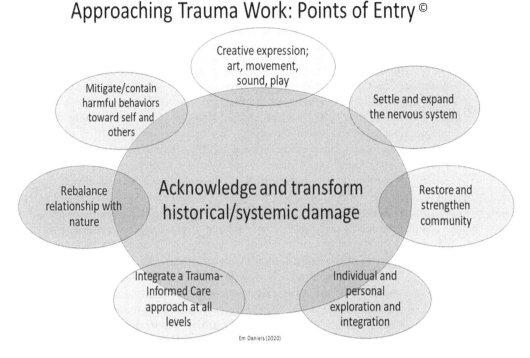

Figure 3.1 Approaching Trauma Work: Points of Entry.

Source: Daniels, M (2020), Spokane WA. Copyright (2020) by M. Daniels. Reprinted with permission.

- **Mitigate/contain harmful behaviors toward self and others:** Current best practices in domestic violence prevention, harm reduction, child safety, and other mental and physical health fields.
- **Culturally responsive practices:** These three Points of Entry fall loosely within Nichols' groupings of race and ethnicity but could be adapted for use across groups

  - Rebalancing relationships with Nature,
  - Restoring and strengthening community, and
  - Individual/personal exploration and integration (which includes any practice primarily impacting the individual, such as movement and spirituality).

- **Creative expression; art, movement, sound, play:** Creative expression has always been a way for people to engage with, express, and release emotional experience. Creative expression can be partnered with or embedded in almost any type of trauma work.
- **Integrate a Trauma-Informed Care approach at all levels:** Pathways for systemic and institutional reform, focused on mental health and harm reduction practices.
- **Settle and expand the nervous system**: Practices that focus on strengthening the connections between the amygdala and pre-frontal cortex, settling the body through directed tasks and activities, including exposure to other settled bodies, and encouraging the nervous system to expand through curiosity and exploration.

- **Acknowledge and transform historical/systemic damage:** Acknowledging and addressing our personal and collective legacies of systemic and historic trauma, understanding that we are an interdependent species living within a planetwide ecosystem.

This approach re-visions what we consider "trauma work" through 1) including a larger number of direct service contact points and 2) expanding our idea of what constitutes a trauma-informed approach. Each element of the diagram can be examined on its own, but none can be separated from our collective historical and systemic trauma. Opening ourselves to the idea that addressing our traumatic experience is necessary for all of us, in more ways than we had previously considered, requires courage and humility.

Menakem notes that "…the human brain always has the capacity to learn, change, and grow. It is genetically designed to mend itself. While trauma can inhibit or block this capacity, the effect is not permanent; once the trauma has ceased and been addressed, growth and positive change become possible once again" (2017, pp. 53–54). Creating an environment that encourages people to settle and expand is a fairly broad approach that can be used in many situations.

It is through introduction of the "soul (or vagus) nerve" (Menakem, 2017; Porges, 2014; van der Kolk, 2014) that we connect the body's physical and chemical responses to fear, through settling, to the state of attentive calm necessary for learning and retrieving information. The soul nerve, which is unlike other nerves, is present in many areas and organs. It is the largest organ in the autonomic nervous system, the system that regulates our most basic functions. Like the amygdala, the soul nerve is a "responder," and connects directly to the brain stem.

It is responsible for spreading feelings and responses throughout the body, whether those are feelings of constriction and self-protection or relaxation and openness. Redirecting our work to settling, which is a way to soothe the soul nerve, also addresses the problem, described by van der Kolk, of "…trying to use the rational brain to talk the emotional brain, ours or others', out of their own reality" (p. 47). Settling the emotional brain is the first step in settling the body, then the rational brain can follow.

As we learn more about how the body remembers traumatic experience and responds to those memories, we see that exerting the rational brain in attempts to control emotional situations rarely leads to a positive outcome. As teachers, the situation worsens if our own emotional responses are activated, catching the most powerful person in the room in an emotional maelstrom. When the person in charge is in the throes of an unanticipated emotional response, the sense of danger and loss of control can spread like wildfire, especially if that person cannot settle themselves.

The reverse is also true. A person who is settled and maintains their internal calm in the face of emotional upset can have a powerful effect on those who might otherwise be caught in the emotional whirlpool. A teacher who remains deeply settled when challenged, or in the face of escalation or emotional disruption, helps their students remain settled. This experience of remaining settled even in the face of upsetting circumstances can provide students with a touchstone they can return to during their own times of upset.

Wounding the Open-Hearted

People love teaching children because children are open-hearted. They are filled with wonder, surprise, and delight. They are more than willing to share those feelings and experiences with everyone. Teachers, especially in preschool and K–3, glow when they talk about the innocence and joy children bring to the classroom. Ideally, children approach learning with vulnerability and curiosity because that is what they know. They haven't retreated into protective shells or developed disconnected coping mechanisms to guard their hearts and minds.

As long as we are unconscious of our own trauma, where it lives and how it presents, we are doomed to continue expressing, in Menakem's words, "dirty pain." "Clean pain" is the pain that comes as we work through our issues, deal with our wounding, and work to heal ourselves. It can hurt, but that hurting is also the pain of growth. "Dirty pain" is the result of denial, and our aversion to facing and healing our wounds (pp. 19–20). Dirty pain is what we inflict when our own pain is touched and activated and we react from those places of raw suffering.

At a certain point, we normalize the pain we inflict on others. We don't consciously experience our behavior and motivations as painful anymore, they are just who we are and how we operate in the world. What were once coping mechanisms we developed to protect us from suffering morph into personalities and behaviors, becoming an unexamined part of our psyche. Research into cultural formation is now considering response to trauma a factor in the formation of cultures themselves.

There is no magic potion that removes the need for us to do the hard work to acknowledge and understand our own traumatic experiences and that is a hard thing for anyone in helping professions to hear. We all want to believe that our desire to help others inoculates us against causing harm, but we are wrong. Good intentions do not negate bad impacts, no matter how much we might wish otherwise. I believe one of the reasons we are so resistant to hearing about harm that happens in learning is because our shame and guilt over causing that harm feels unbearable.

It has taken me many years to recognize and articulate that becoming a teacher does not bestow enlightenment or even self-awareness. The decision to teach does not include a directive to deal with our own traumas and programming and that lack calls for serious deliberation. As long as teachers are not expected and encouraged to address their own combination of power, privilege, and pain, they will continue to perpetuate toxic dynamics and harmful structures across generations.

Educational Trauma

The phrase "educational trauma," as defined by Dr. Lee Ann Gray (2019), introduces the idea that harm happening in educational spaces is of far greater scope and impact than we realize. Educational trauma—emotional and spiritual wounds inflicted during the process of learning, as students are shamed for HOW they learn—is almost certain to embed itself at the core of the learner self. This wounding translates into "you are a bad person because you cannot learn in this specific way, or to this particular standard, regardless of your needs as a learner."

We have no measurement for educational trauma in either adults or children. We are teetering on the edge of articulating its presence and influence, with minimal understanding of its impacts on learning and behavior. Even with so little knowledge, anyone who has worked with adult learners has witnessed the shame, confusion, embarrassment, and defensiveness students display as they try to engage as learners, only to rediscover feelings of failure and worthlessness. Our hearts break over and over, as we feel their intense pain and hopelessness, born from their conviction that who they are as learners is wrong.

Gray uses Alice Miller's work on poisonous pedagogies (2002) as a foundational tenant of educational trauma. Poisonous pedagogy is "…doing harm to children in service of raising them with good character, skills, and values" (2019, p. 65). The people doing this harm may have good intentions, believing that they are doing what is in the child's best interest but in Miller's work, we see that mistakes are treated as not a lack of information, skill, or training, or even just human fallibility. Mistakes mean you are a bad person; fundamentally worthless and irredeemable.

In this environment, mistakes are risky, and must be avoided. Admitting to a mistake means we admit we are bad people. No one wants to think of themselves as a bad person, so we have entangled the necessary process of making mistakes in learning with morality and character. With such high stakes, the classroom quickly becomes a dangerous place. Worthlessness and fundamental "badness," reinforced through public domination and shaming, must be avoided.

Shame is a poisonous, insidious emotion. It strikes to the core of our hearts and lodges at the root of our self, arising to crush our feelings of worth and confidence. It is inevitable that being shamed for who we are as learners and how we understand the world would lead to intense struggles between our innate desire to learn and our desperation to avoid feeling shame. The wounds created by this conflict extend across families and generations. Once people leave school, there are few other structured opportunities for them to detangle these concepts, so the act of learning something new or contradictory becomes a serious threat to the core identity, not just an academic exercise.

Recognizing and naming educational trauma matters because its influence is pervasive and long-standing. Harm done in educational environments goes to the foundation of how we think about and experience ourselves as learners. When our ability to learn is critically wounded, our belief in ourselves as human, capable of joy and growth and expansion, may also be critically wounded. If we do not believe we are capable of learning and changing, how can we ever be different than this person who deserved such harm in the first place?

I cannot overstate the need for corrections educators to examine and address their own educational trauma. In classrooms, that harm is most often replicated when teachers feel threatened or challenged, afraid that we've made a mistake or were wrong. Without direct intervention, the interlocking structures of Dominator relationships, the exclusionary Euro-white knowledge framework, and banking-style education combine in all of us to inflict harm, usually through making others look small and weak. In carceral spaces, where appearing strong is necessary for survival, shaming someone can have serious consequences for their well-being, and will not be tolerated or ignored.

Shame is a dangerous emotion to activate. People will do almost anything to avoid feeling shame because no one wants to feel bad about themselves as a person. This is a critical piece of understanding for adult educators, especially those working with incarcerated or formerly incarcerated students: People who have been shamed as learners, no matter how strong or capable they seem, may have incredibly tender learner selves. Those learner selves are hypersensitive to any perceived threat and have very low tolerance for any perceived criticism. Their defenses against both of these situations are likely to be well-developed and active until they feel some measure of confidence.

Neglecting our own learner self may result in it becoming brittle and unyielding, unable to flex and learn, and make space for others as they grow and stretch. We hide behind our expertise and power, continuing the cycle of educational harm. I've been on all three sides of this toxic triangle: the student who challenges, the teacher who feels threatened, and the observers (usually other students) in the room. Each role is demoralizing and everyone leaves feeling anxious and wary.

Feeling challenged is a fraught situation for most educators. Whether adults teaching children or adults teaching other adults, feeling challenged can quickly arouse our worst selves. It is easy to feel ashamed when our level of confidence is low and we are impatient to get back to our familiar level of confidence. If we are used to being the highly competent expert, it can be difficult to navigate feeling less competent.

In part, this is natural as we learn a new skill. In part, it is our own educational trauma being triggered, as we feel shame for not learning more quickly, or not already being perfect at this new thing. We are so conditioned to avoid feeling and addressing our own pain, however, that it becomes much easier to blame the students for being bad students than to face our own negative self-perception. In the United States, we have deprioritized the talent, skill, and hard work necessary to be a highly competent teacher focusing instead on content expertise and advanced degrees.

Competence in teaching requires the same level of dedication as any other endeavor. My opinion, which is biased, is that teaching requires even greater work and commitment. The damage done by incompetent or malicious teachers is profound, widespread, and inter-generational. We currently treat teaching adults as a throwaway occupation, something anyone can do if they get tired of working in their field. They can always go teach! Now, at a time when education feels vital to protecting our future and the future of the planet itself, we have the chance to reclaim teaching as a calling, not just an occupation.

Adult-Onset Trauma

To this point, we have discussed only traumatic experiences that happen during childhood, but adults also experience traumatic events and we have even less research on the impacts of those experiences on learning. According to Boulanger, who writes from a psycho-analysist's perspective about adult-onset trauma through the lens of mass psychic trauma (i.e., war, acts of terrorism, natural disasters, pandemics), a survivor of adult-onset trauma is faced with a range of experiences from dissociation, to the experience of "living between two deaths," to loss (with recovery not guaranteed) of the experience of self-cohesion (Boulanger, 2011).

Our lack of understanding of adult-onset trauma does not change that it happens, although how it links to the disruptions from childhood is fuzzy. I think of childhood trauma as impacting the foundations of identity and interaction, where adult-onset trauma shakes and cracks the structures we've built to help us navigate the world. Coping structures built to protect or disguise a weakened emotional or cognitive foundation could prove more sus-ceptible to the stress of adult-onset trauma. Even people who are able to recover from trauma fairly smoothly are changed by how they integrate each experience. I have seen people unable to orient themselves to any learning, even after months of effort, but I have also seen adult learners quickly orient (or re-orient) themselves toward learning once they experienced a minimum of settling and connection.

Most educators are familiar with the trajectory of failure in traditional classrooms and organized education. We know, intimately, the amount of effort necessary to convince students to stay focused when they are initially unable to reconnect as learners. We also know that if the student won't allow themselves to redirect early on, the likelihood that they give up increases. Before I started training teachers in trauma-responsive practice, I heard so much frustration along the lines of "why can't they just…?" and "no matter what I try…" and "I can't get them to…"

Those statements and questions almost exclusively focus on how to change student be-havior to match the expectations of the teacher or the institution. It is rare that teachers ask why students would continuously exhibit such behavior, especially when it is clear how that behavior affects their learning. I sometimes hear "why" questions but almost never with a true curiosity, or desire to understand what could prompt students to keep making the same mistakes. Almost always, the assumption is that the student "just can't learn…" or "doesn't understand…" or "doesn't care about…" whatever behavior or skill the teacher is expecting.

Without an understanding of disrupted development, or the impacts of trauma on an adult brain, the natural conclusion, grounded in the experiences in organized education that have shaped us as teachers, is that students are disinterested, unmotivated, rebellious, or unwilling to learn how to function in a classroom. Thus, we replicate the educational trauma we suffered and witnessed, continuing the cycle of harm in learning.

Even in this earliest stage of understanding, we can stop ourselves from replicating harm by simply shifting our thinking and assuming the best of our students. We can also investigate our expectations more closely and shift them to better align with our new approach. What might this look like? When we think about expectations in college classrooms, or institutions and systems generally, it is clear that there is a serious gap between those expectations and how trauma impacts learning.

Bill and I developed Figure 3.2 to demonstrate the contradictory nature of educational expectations and the results of trauma on learning, especially in carceral spaces.

When we showed this to audiences and workshop participants, there was often an audible gasp. The contrast between our educational expectations and the negative effects of trauma is stark. The additional layers of prison environments and institutionalization widen the gap, as students struggle with revived educational trauma and the constraints built into carceral spaces.

Ability to Learn

We know that education is critically important for people in terms of personal and community growth, financial and economic mobility, and becoming better stewards of the planet. There are copious amounts of research on learning—which teaching methods work better and why, what types of support are best for different types of students, what content do students need most and how best to teach it, and on and on. This is another area where Bill and I couldn't find the language to describe the concept so we started using ability to learn, and the term has stuck.

A well-developed ability to learn incorporates physical health, psychological strength and resilience, strong internal and external supports, and well-developed pathways connecting the survival center and executive functions. In this scenario, learners are easily able to achieve the state of internal calm that is necessary to engage the executive function to better integrate learning.

It may help to think of ability to learn as a measure of capacity—how much a person can absorb, integrate, and use as an expansive learner; how well they translate experience to learning to knowledge and action focused on creation and expansion, not only survival. The more well-developed the ability to learn, the greater the capacity, and the more growth is possible.

When our ability to learn is compromised, our chance to bring our fullest selves—all of our gifts, talents, skills, curiosity, and care—into the world is also at risk. Our ability to learn about and express the creative energy and potential embodied in each of us is severely compromised when the majority of our being is focused on survival, or just attempting to navigate life's struggles while coping with the after effects of unhealed and unresolved trauma. Trauma not only hinders people's ability to learn, it can cloud their potential and limit their capacity, until it is integrated and resolved.

Overlapping Clusters of Negative Effects

(reinforced by trauma and incarceration)

- Low/no trust or ability to connect
- Limited ability to make meaning of or sequence events and knowledge
- Skewed sense of time; impaired long-term planning and vision
- Low functioning decision-making
- Repressed critical thinking
- Survival level problem solving ability

Created by Em Daniels & William Keizer

Our Expectations of Adult Learners

(reinforced by organized education)

- Engage openly with authority figures
- Connect consequences to life experience; situate knowledge on a logical timeline
- Manage time well and prioritize; set and reach goals based on long-term vision
- Make reasoned, thoughtful decisions
- Think critically and question
- Executive level problem solving ability

Updated 12/25/2020

Bridging the Gap ©

Figure 3.2 Cross-Institutional Expectations.

Source: Daniels, M. and Keizer, W. (2020). Spokane WA. Copyright (2019) by M. Daniels. Reprinted with permission.

Cognition

Cognition is the area of competency most prized by organized education. Strong cognition is valuable and necessary for all types of learning. Cognitive skills are mental skills that are used in the process of acquiring knowledge and in a system that prioritizes the intellect, strong cognitive skills can make learning fast and easy. In this system, weak cognition means learning is harder. In organized education in the United States, strong cognition separates "good" learners from "so so" and "poor" learners.

Four primary cognitive skills are concentration, perception, memory, and logical thinking (or rational thought) and it is likely we can agree that these are foundational skills for almost all types of learning. Problems arise when we target these skills above all others. As noted by Gray (2019), Zelenz (2020), and Schiffmann (2017), standardized testing is an excellent example of how prioritizing one way of understanding can go badly awry. Instead of encouraging students to learn, integrate, and replicate knowledge in ways that align with who they are as learners, standardized testing requires strict adherence to a specific way of learning, retaining, and retrieving information.

Because standardized testing has taken on such significance in organized education, students who are unable to succeed according to its strict requirements (in both intellect and behavior) are often discarded as failures who are unable to learn. When we look at the developmental impacts of trauma, however, we see that even students who otherwise might feel comfortable and excel in the cognitive realm are disadvantaged.

These impacts may be the long-term outcome of childhood trauma, or they may be temporary as a result of events occurring in adulthood. Either way, they have an immediate impact on ability to learn and cognition:

- **Concentration:** Disrupted by hypersensitivity to physical states and surroundings.
- **Perception:** Grounded in fear-based emotional state that is non-conducive to learning.
- **Memory:** Impacted by disrupted neurodevelopment.
- **Logical thinking:** Unavailable from a heightened state of arousal.

I had the good fortune to screen Gilda Sheppard's documentary "Since I Been Down" (Sheppard, 2020) and listen to Kimonte Carter, Andre Parker, and other members of the Black Prisoner's Caucus (BPC) at Stafford Creek Correctional Center's (SCCC) TEACH program talk about the importance of education. These men consider education as liberation, and a tool they have used to increase their health and well-being. They spoke of the importance of memory, perception, reasoning, and problem solving, noting that inability to grow was equivalent to intellectual death.

Clearly, cognition plays a vital role in our existence as a learning species, and it is in our collective best interests to support well-developed cognitive skills in all people. But we must stop prioritizing and isolating these skills, while suppressing other ways of knowing and being. Trauma-responsive practice requires that all ways of understanding be acknowledged and engaged in equal measure.

Emotional Fluency

Combining physiological harm and societal conditioning results in a limited capacity to acknowledge and cope with intense emotions. This lack of capacity does not mean people don't experience less emotion, but they are unable to channel and integrate that experience so that it becomes meaningful. Emotion is painful, or shameful, and attempts to avoid those unwanted or embarrassing feelings lead to harmful coping mechanisms.

van der Kolk tells us that "[t]raumatized people are afraid to feel deeply" (p. 337). Incorporating specific practices designed to support emotional connection, regulation, and fluency are a key element of any trauma-responsive practice. Becoming emotionally fluent means developing our ability to connect—to create and maintain relationships, as well as self-awareness, impulse control, and understanding our impact on others. Some examples of emotional fluency that strengthen connection-making ability are

- Creating and maintaining relationships
- Healthy empathy and strong boundaries
- Compassionate communication
- Ease of emotional expression and integration

Community and Belonging

Establishing healthy connections and meaningful relationships is an important aspect of trauma-responsive practice (Brunzell, Waters, & Stokes, 2015; Perry, 2006; van der Kolk, 2014). For Black and Brown people, community is critical as it is a often key element of how they experience the world and themselves. BIPOC scholars emphasize the importance of belonging, feeling welcomed and cherished by community as both a settling and culturally relevant healing practice (Akbar, 1998; Duran, 2019; Menakem, 2017; Narine, 2016; Ruiz, 2020).

For BIPOC students, re-establishing themselves as valued members of a community may be integral to their settling process, and another way to practice forming relationships and connections. For Indigenous peoples, Jones & Nichols note that harmony and oneness with the Great Spirit is of utmost importance (2013). Duran & Firehammer (2008) write extensively about soul wounding, liberation psychology, and spiritual emancipation as necessary for healing (as opposed to curing) individual, cultural, and historical oppression.

Demanding Resilience

Resilience is a concept that is ubiquitous in organized education. The amount of content that contains instruction on how to build resilience, especially in BIPOC students, is overwhelming. The stories contained in this content usually follow a set progression, similar to the following:

1. Person recognizing student struggles
2. Person/institution helping student with resources
3. Student overcomes checklist of adversities because of resources
4. Student continues to academic success/employment
5. No significant reflection or movement to transform systems

None of the first four elements are wrong, exactly. We should all be helping our students and demanding our institutions do the same. We all need an internal mechanism to help us keep going when things get hard. Resilience is that thing and, like most things, it is a combination of an internal spark—unique to us—and our external circumstances. Resilience is necessary for all life to continue surviving and evolving, and our brains have a built-in capacity to bounce back and thrive. People's ability to cope with trauma is partly a result of inherent resilience, that unique-to-us spark, and partly external supports. Even if we have an incredible amount of internal resilience, lack of external supports can undermine our efforts to cope.

When we refuse to recognize and address the systemic aspect of these stories, we lay the requirement to "be resilient" at the feet of the individual. These stories are also problematic because they center the delivery of resources as a key to building students' resilience without acknowledging the role of institutions as gatekeepers of power for Euro-white, middle-class systems.

When success in organized education is predicated on intergenerational access to resources, then organized education cannot take credit for people succeeding despite its barriers. Even if an institution helps individual students, lack of systemic change indicates its unwillingness to let go of its gatekeeping role. We cannot demand or expect resilience from individuals without naming and actively working to dismantle repressive structures.

Reclamation and Rediscovery

Trauma-responsive educational space offers students, especially those in carceral environments, a way to reclaim themselves as learners. This reclamation is the first step toward rediscovering aspects of themselves they may have thought lost as trauma disrupted and rerouted their development.

Our ability to learn is critical to our survival AND growth as a species. While trauma is part of the human experience, it can significantly impact our ability to learn. How people navigate these impacts is dependent on a combination of external support and resources and, to some degree, internal capacity. These impacts are ubiquitous and profound in people impacted by mass incarceration, but we can transform our practice in ways that encourage and support settling and expansion in any environment and with any students.

References

Akbar, N. (1998). *Know thyself.* Tallahassee, FL: Mind Production & Associates.

Bloom, S. (2007). The sanctuary model of trauma-informed organizational change. *The Source: The National Abandoned Infants Assistance Resource Center, 16*(1), 12–14, 16. Retrieved from https://www.researchgate.net/publication/242222586_The_Sanctuary_Model_of_Trauma-Informed_Organizational_Change

Boulanger, G. (2011). *Wounded by reality.* New York, NY: Routledge.

Brunzell, T., Waters, L., & Stokes, H. (2015). Teaching with strengths in trauma-affected students: A new approach to healing and growth in the classroom. *American Journal of Orthopsychiatry, 85*(1), 3–9.

Burke-Harris M. D. N. (2019). *The deepest well: Healing the long-term effects of childhood adversity.* New York, NY: Mariner Books.

Centers for Disease Control and Prevention. (2021). *CDC-Kaiser ACE study.* Retrieved from https://www.cdc.gov/violenceprevention/aces/about.html

Centers for Disease Control and Prevention. (2020). *What is epigenetics?* Retrieved from https://www.cdc.gov/genomics/disease/epigenetics.htm

Deardorff, J. (2015). *Discrimination during adolescence has lasting effect on body.* Retrieved from: https://news.northwestern.edu/stories/2015/09/discriminationduring-adolescence-has-lasting-effect-on-body

Duran, E. (2019). *Healing the soul wound.* New York, NY: Teachers College Press.

Duran, E., & Firehammer, J. (2008). Liberation psychology as the path toward healing cultural soul wounds. *Journal of Counseling & Development, 86,* 286–295. doi:10.1002/j.1556-6678.2008.tb00511

Freire, P. (1972). *Pedagogy of the oppressed*. New York: Herder and Herder.

Galtung, J. (1969). Violence, peace, and peace research. *Journal of Peace Research, 6*(3), 167–191. Retrieved from https://www.jstor.org/stable/422690?seq=1

Gray, L.-A. (2019). *Educational trauma*. Cham, Switzerland: Palgrave Macmillan.

Hummer, V., Crosland, K., & Dollard, N. (2010). Trauma-informed behavior support: A training & coaching model for caregivers. *2010 Dependency Summit for Florida's Child Protection Communities*. Orlando, FL. Retrieved from https://csbs.uni.edu/sites/default/files/allfiles/Community%20Systems%20and%20Trauma%20Informed%20Care.pdf

Hummer, V., Dollard, N., Robst, J., Armstrong, M., & Crosland, K. (2009). Innovations in implementation of trauma-informed care practices in youth residential treatment: A curriculum for organizational change. *Child Welfare, 89*(2), 79–95.

Jones, B., & Nichols, E. (2013). *Cultural competence in America's schools*. Charlotte, NC: Information Age Publishing.

Kaiser Permanente. (2019). *Funding new research to prevent childhood trauma*. Retrieved from https://about.kaiserpermanente.org/community-health/news/funding-new-research-to-prevent-childhood-trauma

Levy, D. J., Heissel, J. A., Richeson, J. A., & Adam, E. K. (2016). Psychological and biological responses to race-based social stress as pathways to disparities in educational outcomes. *American Psychologist, 71*(6), 455–473. doi:10.1037/a0040322. PMID: 27571526.

Menakem, R. (2017). *My grandmother's hands*. Las Vegas, NV: Central Recovery Press.

Miller, A. (2002). For your own good: Hidden cruelty in child-rearing and the roots of violence. United States: Farrar, Straus and Giroux.

Narine, S. (2016). Sense of identity core to healing from trauma in prison populations. *Windspeaker, 34*(1), 11. Retrieved from https://issuu.com/windspeaker/docs/windspeaker-april-dig-final2

Nittle, N. K. (2018). *How racism affects black and brown students in public schools*. Retrieved from https://www.thoughtco.com/how-racism-affects-public-school-minorities-4025361

Ohio Department of Education. (n.d.). *The impact of trauma on students*. Retrieved from http://education.ohio.gov/Topics/Student-Supports/PBIS-Resources/Trauma-Informed-Schools/The-Impact-of-Trauma-on-Students

Perry, B. D. (2003). *Effects of traumatic events on children*. Retrieved from https://fa-sett.no/filer/perry-handout-effects-of-trauma.pdf

Perry, B. D. (2006). Fear and learning: Trauma-related factors in the adult education process. *New Directions for Adults and Continuing Education, 110*, 21–27.

Perry, B. D. (2014). *The cost of caring: Secondary traumatic stress and the impact of working with high-risk children and families*. Retrieved from https://ovc.ojp.gov/sites/g/files/xyckuh226/files/media/document/sts_impact_on_child_advocates-508.pdf

Porges, S. W. (2014). *Clinical insights from the polyvagal theory: The transformative power of feeling safe (Norton series on interpersonal neurobiology)*. New York, NY: W.W.Norton.

Raphael, B., Wilson, J., Meldrum, L., Bedosky, C., & Sigman, M. (2000). Preventing PTSD in trauma survivors. *Bulletin of the Menninger Clinic, 64*(2), 181–196. Retrieved from https://www.proquest.com/openview/ca0d772506100ec4d1158e91b8776000/1?pq-origsite=gscholar&cbl=1818298

Ruiz, E. (2020). Structural trauma. *Meridians: Feminism, Race, Transnationalism* (Forthcoming), *20*(2), 1–15. Retrieved from https://philarchive.org/archive/RUZST

Sakala, L. (2014). *Breaking down mass incarceration in the 2010 census: State-by-state incarceration rates by race/ethnicity*. Retrieved from https://www.prisonpolicy.org/reports/rates.html

Schiffmann, T. (2017). *How trauma impacts the brain of adult learners*. Retrieved from https://www.tracyschiffmann.com/blog/how-trauma-impacts-brains-adults.

Schiffmann, T. (2017). *Make your learning environment safe and productive for trauma-impacted learners*. Retrieved from https://www.tracyschiffmann.com/blog/make-environment-safe

Sheppard, G. (2020). *Since I been down* (Motion Picture). Retrieved from https://www.sinceibeendown.com/

United States Census Bureau. (2021). *Quick facts United States*. Retrieved from https://www.census.gov/quickfacts/fact/table/US/PST045219

van der Kolk, B. (2014). *The body keeps the score.* New York, NY: Penguin Books.

Walker, S. (2014). *Trauma informed CARE and practice (powerpoint file).* Retrieved from https://www.slideserve.com/walker-santiago/trauma-informed-care-and-practice

Weinhold, J. (2015). *The long-term effects of adverse childhood experiences.* Retrieved from https://coprofdevcenter.org/the-long-term-effects-of-adverse-childhood-experiences/

Zelenz, S. (2020). *RootEd.* Las Vegas, NV: Zelenz Consulting Group.

A Note on Chapter 4

I wrote this book, in part, because training available to non-prison staff is inconsistent, at best, and does not include the cultural translation and environmental adjustments necessary for educators. A practical guide to teaching inside was the seed idea for this book, so I was shocked when I started hitting a wall writing this chapter. Why was this chapter so hard? What was so difficult about simply describing this environment, and offering advice on the day-to-day of working in a carceral space?

There are two reasons. One is practical—carceral spaces are simultaneously identical and entirely individual. They are identical in purpose, tasked with caging and subordinating people involved with the criminal legal system, and almost indistinguishable in culture. The shared purpose and culture make carceral spaces familiar, the nooks and crannies of para-military bureaucracy are home to individuality. Offering guidance without getting into specific detail became tricky, full of over-explanations and too many modifiers.

I am not an expert on the prison or jail you will be working in, nor am I an expert on all types of prison pedagogy and learning, program creation, curriculum development, or the myriad other facets of education inside. Even though I freely acknowledge my limitations, it feels risky to write broadly about corrections, and I know that I have much room for error.

The second reason, is simple—I hate prisons.

I hate their purpose, the toxic, life-destroying culture, the immense harm perpetuated on every person and piece of land associated with their existence, how they breed suspicion and distrust of learning, continue our legacy of slavery, and poison our society.

In my heart, I am deeply afraid that writing this text is normalizing a thing that must never be normalized. I constantly ask myself if it is moral to write in a neutral tone about a system designed for cruelty; to treat it as normal and mundane in detailing the day-to-day environment and routines.

Ultimately, it is our responsibility to do everything in our power to both help people who are impacted by mass incarceration and work toward its end. Refusing to give people the information they need to have the most impact is a disservice to everyone who needs help. It is also a disservice to individual people trying to do good work in a bad system, and for people living in prisons who may gain some benefit from their time inside.

DOI: 10.4324/9781003048312-102

Chapter 4

Learning and Teaching in Harshly Controlled Environments

In 2003, Angela Davis wrote that the thought of prison abolition was considered too idealistic, too implausible for most people. She writes that this denial is "…a measure of how difficult it is to envision a social order that does not rely on the threat of sequestering people in dreadful places designed to separate them from their communities and families". The conversation about prison abolition has gained in strength, and there is a growing field of research and resources on its practicality and necessity notably Kaba (2021) and Love (2019).

Other than surviving incarceration, there is nothing that can prepare you for teaching in a prison. To some extent, this book may change that but nothing I can write will fully convey the mental and emotional impact of being physically present, day to day, in a place whose primary purpose is to lock people in cages. Mass incarceration and the corrections culture that has evolved with it are toxically co-dependent. Incarceration dehumanizes incarcerated people as well as people who incarcerate and the enabling society, in an ongoing cycle of pain and brutality. To survive in these systems as an educator, you will have to traverse an environment that directly contradicts the purpose of education and often punishes the qualities we encourage and expect our students to develop.

Why would anyone want to teach in such places?

Your answer to this question is important, and will keep you focused during hard moments. You should be clear on your answer before you set foot inside any facility. Working in these harsh spaces, immersed in corrections culture, witnessing the level of harm done to incarcerated people and those who incarcerate is arduous and debilitating. There will be days when you feel like every decision compromises a part of your soul. Those are the days when the answer to this question will either keep you going or let you know it's time to leave.

My answer to that question started as curiosity about people who work in prisons, and in needing a job. It developed into wanting the women I taught to learn as much as possible, so they could decide what kind of life they wanted to build for themselves. I wanted them to learn in an environment where it was expected that they would ask questions, challenge each other, hold each other to account, and give each other grace in rough moments.

I believe that we built that space together. I can say with certainty that every student who spent time in my classroom worked to their capacity and put forth their best effort. I can say that about myself, although I also look back and see many missteps. I have come to understand that my experience teaching in prison was unique. I had a level of freedom from oversight that is almost unthinkable today, and was able to emphasize building relationships and connection as a central theme of my teaching. I have never been able to find the right words to describe my experience, but I will always feel honored by the women who chose to take that journey with me.

The educator in me answers that question with "everyone deserves to experience themselves as capable, competent learners, no matter the circumstance." The justice advocate

DOI: 10.4324/9781003048312-4

in me answers that question with "people who have been the most harmed are the people who are most capable of helping us learn to do things differently, if they so choose."

This chapter is written as a guide to 1) who is in your classrooms, building your classroom container, power and culture dynamics, and the absolute necessity for self-reflection and care and 2) the general structure and organization of carceral institutions, corrections culture, and how both of these affect your classroom space and experience.

From this point, we will focus on working and teaching in carceral environments. My experience was in a women's minimum security prison, with some work in the co-located medium security facility. I have learned through conversation with other prison educators and formerly incarcerated students that my experience was unique, and that I had an almost unheard-of level of freedom and autonomy in my classroom. While I believe this freedom, when recognized, contributed to my exit from that position, it is important to note that I write from an experience that you may not share.

I write as accurately as possible in hopes it will help you avoid some of the problems I encountered, and better resolve the issues you cannot avoid. It is also my hope that you will remember that you are teaching people—human beings like yourself with hopes, dreams, ambitions, and loved ones—not felons, convicts, offenders, adults in custody, or any of the other labels used by the system to dehumanize and belittle. It has been a long path and immense learning to feel I could write this and do justice to the topic.

In this chapter, I use the words "facility" and "prison" as shorthand for any type of carceral space. Every facility is so different that I have tried to keep my descriptions and statements broadly applicable, but they are still based on my personal experience. I do not think any single text can provide a comprehensive guide to every different type of facility, program, or teaching approach, but this should give you a starting point, including what questions might be most helpful.

Who Are Our Students?

Incarcerated people are our community members. They are our family, friends, and neighbors, with 45% of households reporting at least one incarcerated member (Enns, Yi, Comfort, Goldman, Lee, Muller, & Wildeman, 2019). They are BIPOC, have disabilities, and over two-thirds are incredibly poor, existing on less than $12,000 a year prior to incarceration (Alexander, 2012).

The vast majority of people who are locked up are in either state prisons or local jails. Most people in jails are being held in pre-trial detention, unable to afford bail, sometimes spending months or years awaiting trial. Roughly 97% of incarcerated people will return to their communities, whether or not they can get the support they need to restabilize their lives.

> **Box 4.1   A caution about ACEs scores**
>
> I am using the average ACE score because it is 1) currently an accepted quantifiable measure of traumatic experience, and 2) a way to better understand how trauma is connected to incarceration.
>
> Under NO circumstances should non-mental-health professionals attempt to discover someone's score or use that score and related information for any purpose.
>
> One of the major criticisms of the ACE score is that it would become a screening tool and, potentially, fall into general usage as such. Unfortunately, this scenario is becoming more and more common, despite the possible re-traumatization of people required to answer the ACEs questions to receive services.

Most do not have a high school credential, but do have severe educational trauma, one thread in complex and long-term trauma histories. The average person in the United States scores between one and three on the ACE questionnaire, while incarcerated people average a six, with no consideration of historic or systemic trauma, or trauma encountered as adults.

In all of my years working with incarcerated and formerly incarcerated students, I have yet to meet a student who had not been involved with the foster system, and the majority had dropped out of middle or high school. Many have serious health issues, substance use disorders and, from a lay person's perspective, all have some version of post-traumatic stress, compounded with what they were suffering prior to incarceration and whatever terrible things happened to them during incarceration. Many of my students had disabilities; most had some type of undiagnosed learning disability.

Women are the fastest-growing incarcerated population, with a 600+% increase over the last 15 years, and women's paths to prison are different than men's. If you are teaching women, it is statistically likely that most of your students are mothers, have substance use and mental health issues, have been involved in abusive relationships, and potentially are victims of trafficking. Most commit crimes of poverty such as identity theft, check fraud, or non-violent drug offenses, which were considered misdemeanors until they were swept up in harsher sentencing initiatives in the 1990s–2000s (Wartenweiler, 2017).

Of the students I have worked with, both inside the prison and on a college campus, maybe 10% were returning to a safe home and had strong family support. It may be less than that, but it isn't more. Of those other 90%, some were going back to the same location and people who were involved in their pre-incarceration lives. Some were returning to temporary or transitional housing, with no place to go after their time ran out. Some were returning to a hotel room, paid up for a few days, some released straight to a shelter, or to the street.

Incarceration is one intergenerational consequence of historic and systemic racism, poverty, misogyny, and violence. Our students are parents of children who are 50% more likely to see the rotting interior of the pipeline to prison than children of the unincarcerated. I remember the first time a student came to me, so excited, and told me that their parent had been assigned a bunk next to them, exclaiming, "We're bunkies now!" I didn't respond because how do you celebrate intergenerational co-incarceration?

While most of us would claim, without hesitation or question, that education benefits everyone, the school-to-prison pipeline stands as a blatant rebuke to that claim. The connection between "poor" performance in organized education (as early as third grade) and later involvement in with the criminal legal system has been clearly established for years (Union, American Civil Liberties, n.d.) but in practice, what does this really mean in corrections classrooms?

The most far-reaching and comprehensive report on corrections education is from the Bureau of Justice Statistics. The report was completed in 2003 and is now quite old, but results state that roughly 68% of people entering state prison had not completed their high school diploma (Harlow, 2003). Tragically, this figure appears to have changed little (see Table 4.1), and still aligns with more recent research and reporting on the school-to-prison pipeline.

Further data from the BJS 2003 report show that "about 26% of State prison inmates said they had completed the GED® while serving time in a correctional facility, and 68% of State prison inmates did not receive a high school diploma." State prison inmates who had not completed high school or the GED® included the following groups:

Table 4.1 Educational attainment for correctional populations and the general population

	Total Incarcerated Population	State Prison	Federal Prison	Local Jail Population	Probation Population	General Population
Education						
Some high school or less	41%	40%	27%	47%	31%	18%
GED	23%	29%	23%	14%	11%	Not available
High school diploma	23%	21%	27%	26%	35%	33%
Postsecondary	13%	11%	24%	14%	24%	48%

40% of males and 42% of females
27% of whites, 44% of blacks, and 53% of Hispanics
52% of inmates 24 or younger and 35% of inmates 45 or older
61% of noncitizens and 38% of US citizens
59% with a speech disability
66% with a learning disability, and 37% without a reported disability
47% of drug offenders 12% of those with military service and 44% with no military service.

Based on the statistics, an incarcerated student has a good chance of being poor, a BIPOC male, between 30–40 years of age. They will have an extensive, complex personal trauma history including historic and systemic oppression, long-term contact with foster care and legal systems beginning in middle or high school, low educational attainment (i.e., lack of high school credential), and a substance use disorder, untreated mental health needs, and possibly a traumatic brain injury (TBI). If they are a woman, there is an 85% chance they are a primary parent or caregiver.

A note of interest and a data point that is missing from the BJS report is the higher incidence of TBIs among incarcerated people. By some accounts, "…studies note that 25–87% of inmates report a history of traumatic brain injury (TBI), in contrast to a TBI-prevalence rate of 10–38% in the general U.S. population" (Enns et al., 2019). Not only do these injuries complicate treatment and wellness, they may interfere with the person's ability to learn across their lifespan. Without assistance, it seems less and less likely that these students will regain abilities necessary to succeed in education and employment.

Education in prison has the same potential as education in free spaces: it can do great good or great harm. One of the biggest challenges corrections educators face is working with students who have already suffered enormous harm in educational spaces. For some, the desire to learn and grow may overcome their fear. For others, the desire may not be able to immediately overcome years of defenses. For others, the choice to be in a classroom may not have been theirs, and their past trauma rises to meet their current fear and resentment, giving them no space to reach out. Still others may have no connection to education at all, having come from communities or families that saw little for them beyond a shovel or wheelbarrow.

I come from a "first generation out of poverty" family that claimed to value education. Although both parents made their way out of their impoverished childhoods, neither had an understanding of what "getting an education" required, or how to help me do such a thing. I remember being punished for reading too much in third grade, teacher cruelty and apathy in middle and high school, and harshly dogmatic instructors in college. I went to college immediately after high school graduation, stayed for a year and left—a familiar story for many first-generation students.

No one asked me what I wanted to do, where I saw myself in five years, or even helped me connect "getting an education" to something I could do or be. It took almost 20 years before I completed my undergraduate and master's degrees. I've been a student in almost every type of educational setting, taught in most of them, and this educational meandering has had a very specific benefit: My experiences with how people learn are not confined to one type of teaching or one type of student.

My background is helpful on a practical level, but also provided a way to continually assess how people learn and seek patterns in that learning. From my first experience teaching, during the Welfare to Work 90s, I knew there was something that interfered with adult learning—something beyond the distractions and stress of everyday life—something beyond conscious control. When I first began teaching inside, even with a large tool bucket of skills and strategies, I constantly fell back on trial and error. I knew there was a common barrier, but its name and shape remained hidden.

According to Gray (2019), the spectrum of educational trauma, which includes standardized testing, bullying, and chemical restraints (often used on students diagnosed with ADHD, many who may be diagnosed incorrectly), is a major factor in students' entry into the prison pipeline. Her work also notes that students who are chemically restrained may, after they exit school (with or without a diploma) be suffering withdrawals as they no longer have access to those medications. Those withdrawal symptoms may result in students seeking relief through usage of other drugs. It is not a big leap to connect this possibility with the high rates of substance use disorder present in system-impacted people, especially when combined with the likelihood of other traumatic experience.

Gray notes that "...the place where education and trauma intersect, negatively impacting communities and people, is in school. Educational trauma is the cycle of harm inadvertently perpetuated in schools" (p. 44), and while I agree with this basic premise, it does not go far enough. In the United States, schools are not passive places of intersection; they are active gatekeepers for multiple systems of domination and oppression. Schools and foster care are parallel entry points into the prison pipeline, most notably for BIPOC and disabled children (Menakem, 2017).

I am certain that every student I interacted with in prison, alternative high schools, and community-based organizations carried the scars of educational harm. While they were physically adults, with needs of adult learners, their experiences in the classroom and with formalized learning were minimal. But that lack of exposure became a minor concern as the larger problem took shape: these students had little to no confidence in their ability to learn.

This chapter and the next focus on the practicalities of teaching in prison and building a trauma-responsive practice even in harsh conditions. The foundation of building such a practice is treating people with grace and dignity—regardless of the circumstances. Aside from the day-to-day of teaching inside, the majority of my recommendations for setting up boundaries, building classroom environment, managing relationships with students, and dealing with disciplinary issues are grounded in treating your students (and yourself) with dignity at all times. When the premise of every decision you make is that all people are worthy of being treated well, and their humanity acknowledged, you can bring dignity into even the worst situations.

Carceral Spaces

Prisons and jails are places of great despair and, occasionally, great opportunity. The opportunity is the amount of time adults have to focus on learning and education, when it is available. There are few other environments where assuming the worst is the norm, and kindness and care are instantly suspect. Whatever the environment, circumstances, or behavior, your priority is to treat people with dignity, and humanize those who may have dehumanized themselves.

When I applied for a job in the prison, I had no idea what I was doing. I didn't realize I was applying to work inside a prison, and I had no understanding of corrections or prison education. Even as I was going on a tour of the facilities, it didn't quite sink in that I would be working here every day, behind rolls and rolls of razor wire, fencing, reinforced cement walls, and huge sliding steel doors. I remember only snippets of my first day—getting my picture taken for my badge, then finding out the color of shirt I wore was the same color as the sweatshirts women were given when they were "in trouble." I never had that picture retaken.

The learning curve was steep, especially since training for non-DOC staff had been eliminated before I started. My co-workers and dean helped me with the day-to-day, although none of them had much to say about the culture of corrections. There was one other person on the education staff who had been there less than 10 years, most were at 15 or more. No one truly remembered what it was like to be new to working in prison, and many of my colleagues had accepted and normalized the culture. Some had been there so long they had become de facto corrections staff, committed to corrections culture and norms.

There are three main jurisdictions of adult corrections entities and they match the jurisdictions of law enforcement: local (counties, cities, or other municipalities), state (most often designated as the [STATE] Department of Corrections (DOC)), and the Federal Bureau of Prisons (BOP). There is a lot of crossover between these entities, with a large percentage of people cycling between jail and state prison, and a smaller population moving between federal and state facilities. Private prisons and juvenile "rehabilitation" facilities (not those run by local, state, or federal bodies) contract with these jurisdictions, even though they are subject to almost no oversight and few private facilities offer education.

Youth (or juvenile) corrections entities are similar, although youth are considered a "special" population that requires special care. Youth designations are often 21 and under, although some states (like Washington) have moved the upper limit to 24 or 25. Whether or not a youth is actually tried and convicted as a youth is dependent on the charges assigned by the District Attorney (DA), the county's lead prosecutor. Depending on the state, certain charges may automatically result in a juvenile being assigned into the adult system, where they may be tried, convicted, and incarcerated as an adult.

Even if youth are tried and convicted in the youth system, most states still hand down extremely long or life sentences for certain convictions. One consequence of this practice is that people convicted, for example, at age 15 and who receive a sentence of 15 years would age out of the youth system at 25. At that point, they would be transferred to the adult system, where they would serve the remaining years.

My experience with youth is not inside prison but at an alternative high school. "Alternative high schools" is a broad designation that is applied to schools that serve young people who have not done well in the typical environment of organized education. Sometimes, these schools are a secure (or locked-down) facility and students are mandated by the juvenile system to be there. Non-secure schools may also serve students mandated to attend by juvenile justice systems, although those students have more freedom than those in locked-down schools.

State prisons for adults are often (though not always) located in remote, rural communities and may be a significant source of jobs and security for those communities. Locating prisons in remote areas has consequences that include difficulty finding staff and longer distances for friends and families to travel to visit loved ones, which can have a devastating impact. This practice can also contribute to prison gerrymandering, a way to increase population counts in sparsely populated areas that we will discuss in more depth.

Jails are more representative of local policing practices, and BIPOC populations and poor and disabled people are over-represented in most jails. Jails (youth and adult) are located inside city and county lines, and the city and county may share facilities or not, depending on need. In Washington, for example, jails are considered short-term facilities, intended for sentences of 365 days or less, state prison for sentences of a year and day or longer. In practice, people can spend months or years in jail, awaiting trial, because they cannot afford, or were not offered, bail. There are states where jails are also used for longer-term sentences, and are considered part of the state's corrections system.

Facilities mostly fall into "secure" or "non-secure" designations. Secure facilities are designed to physically isolate people from society. Full physical isolation, as we have conceived it, translates into tiny living spaces behind locked metal doors, inside larger locked concrete and metal buildings that are behind miles of concrete, metal, barbed, and razor wire fencing that constitute a secure perimeter. Non-secure facilities have some similarities, such as locked doors, controlled entry and exit, and strictly enforced behavior, but they do not have secure perimeters. With a few exceptions, adult facilities, at the date of this writing, do not allow Internet access and strictly limit communication with and access to the free world.

Most secure facilities are designated for certain custody levels that include Minimum, Medium, and Maximum. The federal system includes Super Max prisons, which rely heavily on segregation and solitary confinement, confining people who will likely not be returning to society. Within facilities, there are also different levels of security and confinement ranging from work camps, where people may have access to outside employment and few restrictions inside, to close custody and solitary confinement.

Close custody is a high level of security for people who are deemed to require direct, armed supervision. Solitary confinement (also called "the hole" or "Special Housing Unit" (SHU)) is 23 hours a day with no human contact beyond, at best, a supervised hour outside in a caged area. People are sent to solitary for many reasons including behavior, a need for high level of safety via isolation (which includes health-related circumstances), prison politics, or while awaiting the outcome of an investigation or other decisions.

You may find yourself working in any combination of these, although access to teach people in higher levels of custody is less frequent. Before you accept a position, you should familiarize yourself with the custody level(s) of the facility, be clear about where you will spend the majority of your time, and where your office and classroom are located.

The environment of the prison, which includes facility culture and practice, staff attitudes, and level of security can influence what and how you teach. Never forget that the system itself is not friendly to education, especially education intended to liberate and expand the mind. **Your** worst-case scenario might be that you aren't allowed back into the facility to teach, but your students cannot leave. Although we must continue to engage in liberatory educational practice, part of your responsibility is to do this in a way that minimizes risks to your students, yourself, and your program.

This is not to discourage anyone from working in a particular security level, but to encourage you to inform yourself about the physical environment where you may be spending a great deal of time. Mixed-custody facilities are common (i.e. Maximum and Medium custody in the same compound) and may be co-located with a Minimum custody facility or work camp. Part of understanding your job is knowing where you will be assigned to teach. Your interview process should include a tour of the facility, including where you will be working, and that is the perfect time to ask questions.

Halfway houses and work releases (both state and federal) are two common types of transitional living. They may be run by the corrections entity itself, or operations may be contracted out to a private company. Even if operations are contracted out, there will be security staff onsite to handle custody-related issues, as people living there may still be considered *in custody* although not in a secure facility. These facilities can be located anywhere, although they are usually close to an urban are where some support is available as people release.

Whether adults at halfway houses and work releases can receive education during their stay is dependent on state law, the technical definition of the transition house, and how the DOC or BOP runs the facility. Policy and practice are often misaligned and while the public message may be that people can attend school while in a transitional house, practice and systemic barriers (such as lack of Internet access and restrictions on funding) may prevent people from attending. Corrections culture is also steeped in "work release = employment above all" and convincing security staff to allow people to attend school can prove a significant challenge.

Carceral spaces are part of a complex, interlocked system of crime and punishment that includes legislators, law enforcement, the courts, incarceration, education, economics, politics, and communities. Each of these points in the cycle is a complicated bureaucracy in its own right, and they do not work well together. When you work in any of these spaces, learning the requirements of the bureaucracy is part of why the learning curve is so steep. Who does what, what forms and paperwork have to be filed when, who has to be notified and why and how, what you are required to do and when and how—this part of teaching in prison is tedious, at best. Learning how to operate in the system gives you both space and protection to teach, but also normalizes what should not be normalized.

No matter how comfortable and familiar you become with your classroom and students, with the prison where you teach, do not normalize that you teach in a place designed to put human beings in cages. You will hear stories, see things, and learn about atrocities happening daily, all things out of your control. It is easy to drop into the extremes of response—debilitating helplessness or full righteous anger. Neither of these is useful while you are inside, so part of your responsibility is to put them aside in the moment, stay settled and focused in your work, then tend to your emotional state in a safe place. Do not neglect this aspect of the work—you maintaining a settled system requires that you deal with what you're exposed to as well as your own emotional needs.

If you are teaching at the community end of corrections, you have a different set of circumstances to consider and your ability to work with people while they are incarcerated in a secure facility may be limited.

Built-in Tensions

There are three major built-in tensions between education and corrections: clashing systems and cultures, untended trauma in both staff and incarcerated people, and ever-present racial and economic conflicts.

Large systems rarely mesh well. Most bureaucracies do not accommodate the needs of other bureaucracies and education and corrections are no exception. Adding to an already complex arrangement, large systems have their own cultures, values, norms, and mores.

Above all, they protect themselves. Bureaucratic systems, like corrections and organized education, are adept at evaluating new elements and assessing whether or not they pose a threat. Some systems, like education, have more tolerance for risk but others, like corrections, have almost none.

On the surface, organized education can easily fit to the corrections environment. Its structure, rules, behavioral expectations, and outcomes appear to align well with correctional claims of "rehabilitation." There is an indication that access to education raises morale and may lower disciplinary incidents, as well as research that supports education in prison as a way to reduce recidivism. These are all in alignment with the public goals of corrections regarding security and safety for both incarcerated people and the general public.

And yet there is a palpable, ongoing strain between prison education programs and corrections. Part of this strain is the clash between system needs. Higher education (and learning generally) require access to information, materials, and, increasingly, technology. Students also need to communicate with their instructors and other students in order to have a rich learning experience. Corrections, with a primary goal of security, does not allow the types of communication most often used in education, nor does it allow freedom of access to information and materials. These are heavy constraints, but prison educators have been working around them for decades.

The other aspect of strain is a fundamental clash in values and purpose. Liberation through learning and personal growth is a foundational value of education. Even with its systemic flaws, education attempts to liberate mind and spirit. That freedom is antithetical to the base nature of a system designed for control and suppression. While it is clear that learning and education are beneficial, control-oriented systems cannot help but resist the presence of freedom-oriented systems, organizations, and people. The best way to navigate this cultural divide is to treat everyone with dignity, know what is expected, and create a transparent decision-making process.

Carceral spaces harm everyone who spends time in them. They create endless cycles of trauma as unresolved pain rebounds from person to person, exacerbating old wounds and causing new. This is true of corrections staff, especially security, as well as incarcerated people. Both groups have seen and experienced people at their worst, and that creates a particular type of harm. For corrections staff, moral injury may be a significant source of personal distress and disease.

Scholars have been discussing the impacts of trauma, primarily in the context of war, civilian, and environmental disasters, for thousands of years. History notes that trauma research began as a way to treat soldiers returning from war. But behaviors we now know are symptoms of severe trauma were often considered a moral failure, and a weakness of character (Substance Abuse and Mental Health Services Administration, 2014). The belief—that people do bad things because they are bad people, and people who get good things must be good people—is thoroughly embedded in our society and culture.

According to Ruiz, "'bad luck' can *make you who you are*, whereas responses to good fortunes reflect who you already are..." This "...*logic of wounding* detaches people from the sets of social, cultural, and epistemic practices that produce them in order to place their lives within a universalized narrative arc of human existence" (emphasis author's) (Ruiz, 2020). These beliefs do not take into account that choices are often dictated by circumstance and resources, nor do they question who is defining the terms "good" and "bad." They are one source of the question "what's wrong with you?" that we so often use when people make decisions we find incomprehensible.

The Moral Injury Project, a group of researchers, veterans, and others from Syracuse University, defines a moral injury as "...the damage done to one's conscience or moral compass when that person perpetrates, witnesses, or fails to prevent acts that transgress one's own moral beliefs, values, or ethical codes of conduct" (The Moral Injury Project, n.d.). Moral injury happens when people are forced to make life and death decisions that may conflict with their self-perception, then cannot integrate those experiences and actions into their idea of themselves. Menakem adds that inflicting harm is, itself, a form of secondary trauma that leads to moral injury. His definition of moral injury notes that "[b]ecause the perpetrator knows that he or she has committed a moral transgression, his or her actions also create profound shame" (Menakem, p. 47).

The moral injury aspect of trauma work surfaces in corrections, as staff often have military or combat histories. They may be in positions to make life and death decisions, and likely made decisions about meeting force with force on a daily basis. It is not entirely accurate to compare prisons and jails to war zones, nor am I suggesting that moral injury of this nature occurs in learning spaces. What I am suggesting is that humans using force to keep other humans in cages, following a rigid code of rules and regulations, inflicts a specific type of harm, one we know little about. This is a crucial piece of information for those working in carceral spaces, understanding that they are proximate to the combined traumatic experience of both incarcerated people and those who do the incarcerating.

Menakem speaks to moral injury as a consequence of white supremacy, as an ongoing experience of shame and increasing trauma in white bodies (Menakem, p. 105). This shame, historic and current, continues to exist and exert tremendous influence on white bodies, especially the bodies of law enforcement, including corrections officers and staff. This matters greatly when we talk about the importance of aggressive self-care, and as teachers learn to navigate such a fraught environment. Prison educators who remain unaware of these dynamics are far more likely to replicate them, continuing to harm the people in their classrooms.

Our third point of built-in tension arises from the historical racial practice of pitting poor white people against Black and Brown people. Close to 60% of correctional officers are white, as well as close to 60% of incarcerated people. Close to 40% of incarcerated people are BIPOC (which is a much higher representation than their percentage in the population). Elites in slave-owning states deliberately created racial tension and resentment in poor whites (Milloy, 2016) and that tension simmers in today's prisons.

The tactic of turning poor people, specifically poor white people and poor Black people, against each other has been used for centuries and has proven just as effective and devastating inside the prison–industrial complex. As an educator, you may find that you run into unexpected or unexplained resistance to basic needs or simple requests—things that no one would think twice about in another environment. But education in prisons isn't necessarily popular, especially for two- or four-year programs. The resentment is real and, as outlandish as it may seem, understandable.

Public resentment against prison education is encapsulated in the question "Why should they get free education? I didn't and my kids don't either!" It is easy to be angry at this question, and at the people asking, but it is a question that demands serious consideration in both substance and context. In this question, we hear the echoes of past and current intersecting conflicts of race and class, complicated by the urban/rural divide and suspicion of education stoked by elite politicians and business owners. This conflict comes into sharper focus when we consider where prisons are located and why, and who benefits from those locations.

The business and economic impacts of mass incarceration are firmly entrenched in all levels of society. Prisons are often built in poor rural areas as an economic stimulator—a plan that never works—but has been a popular political power play for decades. There are significant political gains for politicians in these areas also. Despite state laws, prisoners are almost always counted where they are incarcerated (Levine, 2020; Census Will Continue To Count Prisoners Where They Are Incarcerated, 2018), not at their last known address before imprisonment.

This is known as "prison gerrymandering" and means that for purposes of redistricting and allocation of state and federal funding, people are not counted in their home communities (often urban BIPOC areas), but in poor, rural, largely white areas (Levine, 2018; Prison Gerrymandering Project, 2018). "To an extent that few Americans have yet appreciated, record rates of incarceration have, in fact, undermined our American democracy, both by impacting who gets to vote and how votes are counted" (Thompson, 2013).

Box 4.2   Impacts of prison gerry-mandering

To better understand the real and measurable impacts of prison gerrymandering see:

*   https://www.prisonersofthecensus.org/
*   https://www.thenation.com/article/mark-pocan-gerrymandering-prisons/
*   https://www.nbcnews.com/politics/politics-news/will-prison-gerrymandering-be-next-big-fight-n999656
*   https://www.naacpldf.org/case-issue/prison-based-gerrymandering-reform/

To navigate the resentment from corrections staff against education for incarcerated people, it is helpful to look at the decline of white, rural communities, prison location as perceived economic stimulus, economic benefits of free/cheap labor, and impacts of prison gerrymandering on our democracy.

We make this effort because people who work in these prisons, whether administration, management, or security, are heavily indebted to the system, and will work to protect and defend it, regardless of the cost to themselves, incarcerated people, or the country at large.

Armstrong, Atkin-Plunk, & Wells (2015) note that 31.5% of corrections officers have a high school credential, while 43.8% have some college. Only 20% have a college degree or graduate work. The thought that people convicted of crimes have access to more or better education than they have may be unbearable for some. Making a miserable situation worse is that poor white children who may end up working in prisons have been subject to educational trauma also. Their belief in themselves as learners, as creative beings, has also been undermined and shattered.

Structural racism and white supremacy may have protected them from the public side of the criminal legal system, but have provided a doorway into its destructive interior. Study after study, as well as personal experience and stories from students, friends, and family, demonstrate how the destructive nature of corrections (which is an aspect of law enforcement) infects individuals, families, and communities. Rates of addiction, domestic violence, risky behavior, and suicide are higher, as well as early death rates after retirement.

Far from being the economic engines described by politicians and the prison-industrial complex, prisons and jails are sinkholes of suffering. They absorb and control human and economic capital wherever they are located, but are incapable of creating long-term growth, prosperity, or a sustainable quality of life. The rhetoric of prisons as job engines and instigators of economic viability is deceptive at best and delusional at worst. From the first moment, a prison is a limited, inward-facing, static entity, unable to contribute to growth in its surrounding community. This is true even of for-profit models as they thrive by starving staff and incarcerated people of resources, funneling those savings into the pockets of CEOs and absentee shareholders.

Common Terms

Like every other system and institution, prisons and jails have their own language and vocabulary. These may change across facilities, but you should be able to translate fairly quickly. I'm including only the terms that will most often impact your daily work. If your facility offers training to volunteers and contractors, make sure you understand how each of these is handled and (if possible) get a daily schedule. Understanding this aspect of prison quickly is in your best interest.

Commissary or Canteen

The commissary (or canteen) is the only retail-type option inside prisons (I don't know if they are available in jails). They have a wide range of products, including food, clothing, arts and crafts supplies, pens, pencils, erasers, notebooks, and electronics. Canteen delivery can disrupt schedules, especially during big deliveries that require more time waiting in line, or general disruptions in the schedule. Once people receive their canteen order, they have to go back to their bunk or cell and secure the items. This can take even more time, especially if they have to rearrange their storage area. Remember that they have no choice in when they can pick up their items, so talk with your supervisor about how much flexibility to allow for delays on canteen day.

Movement

Movements are designated times that incarcerated people are allowed to move from one part of a facility to another. Different facilities may be more or less strict with movement times, but there will be times when very few people should be out and about. You may be in a very strict facility, which means people cannot move around until a specific movement time is called, unless there is an emergency. If you are uncertain, speak to your dean or supervisor, or check with the appropriate security staff.

Count

Count time is exactly that—specified times of day where every incarcerated person is counted and their location noted. Count is done several times a day, at specific times, and depending on how quickly it does or does not go, everything else can and does move. You will rarely have anything to do with count but may, on rare occasion, end up with students during late morning count. If this is unplanned, notify the appropriate security personnel immediately. If this is planned, follow your facility procedures to make sure your students are counted properly and your count responsibility is cleared.

Count may be done at different actual times, but it is done five times a day, and a rough schedule is

- Morning (usually before breakfast)
- Late morning (done after morning programming but before people go to lunch)
- Late afternoon (done after afternoon programming but before people go to dinner)

- Evening (before lights out)
- Midnight (most folks are sleeping except graveyard workers)

If you are working during the day, you'll likely only be in the facility for the late morning/lunch count. If you are working in the evening, you may miss count altogether at classes are usually after dinner, and students have to be back at their units before evening count.

If counts do not clear, which can happen for many reasons, they have to be redone. If they take long enough to clear, a facility may require an automatic, more extensive recount. There is nothing you can do about this except stay updated and adjust your class plan for the day. Once count clears, students may come in all at once, or may straggle in depending on how quickly their units released them to chow, and how long it took to eat. It will likely take them a few minutes to settle, especially if count took a long time to clear, as extended counts are disruptive to their daily routines.

Callouts

All facilities use some method to track and share incarcerated people's daily schedules. The prison I worked in used the term "callout" but yours may use something different. Whenever someone has to be somewhere other than their cell or bunk, it is supposed to be noted in the facility's scheduling software/database. There are many types of callouts—standing callouts for work, programming, religious observance, and as-needed callouts to schedule a one-off conversation about grades are all examples. You may or may not be responsible for entering callouts for students to come to your class, but you should know where to go to look at their schedules.

Callouts are printed at least once daily, and copies are given to everyone who has people on a callout for that day. Callout sheets are also printed and posted in the tiers, units, or dorms so everyone can see where they are supposed to be that day, and when. Callouts are extremely important for two reasons: 1) it is a way to document where every incarcerated person is supposed to be during the day, and who is responsible for them during that time and 2) it is the only way incarcerated people know where they are officially supposed to be and when.

People with jobs or education, for example, should see themselves on the callout for those activities daily. With a few exceptions, any time someone has to go somewhere away from their unit or dorm, they should be on a callout. It is the responsibility of each department to schedule callouts for people as needed. This happens in Education and is usually handled by a program coordinator or administrative support staff. Attendance gets matched to callouts and attendance is a critical number for Education funding.

If you have access to the facility database, you may be able to see a student's daily callouts and determine their location, or at least contact the callout coordinator, if they don't show up for class. If you don't have direct access to this information or are a volunteer, you can try calling their unit or tier officer to find out where they are. Your supervisor or volunteer coordinator should let you know before your first class how callouts are handled and who should get them after they are noted for attendance. This is another task only your or another staff member can handle—**do not** ask your students or clerks to handle or deliver callout sheets.

You will not see copies of callouts or be notified (other than informally) that someone has been ordered to report elsewhere instead of your classroom, no matter that the student needs to take a critical exam or participate in an important group presentation. If students don't show up, checking their callouts should always be your first action.

Medical callouts: Medical appointments routinely take priority over other types of appointments, in part because wait times can be very long if people need to see dentists, specialists, or be taken to a hospital. You will not be notified if students have medical callouts, even if those callouts conflict with something you consider important, so have backup plans ready for test or presentation days.

Pill Line

I truly do not know the real name for this so I'm going to call it the pill line. I'm hesitant to give many details and only mention it because it is likely to impact your class if several people have to leave. Medical dispenses medication once or twice a day. They cannot go around to all the living areas, so people are on callouts and they come to the medical dispensing area, stand in a line, take their meds, and then get their mouths checked by security before they leave. Other people get a supply of something non-prescribed, like allergy medication, which they may need to take back and put in their living area.

Your students will know if it's a day for pill line, so just plan accordingly.

Structure

With some understanding of the larger field of corrections, we turn our attention to how these systems are arranged and where education programs are typically placed. If you are feeling confused and uncertain about why I'm writing about all of this, I understand. It doesn't seem immediately relevant to your work and for some, maybe it isn't. So why am I sharing it with you? Because every decision you make as a teacher can have a cascading set of unintended consequences for your students, their quality of life, and potentially their release date. Because you are staff, you inhabit a position of authority over your students, and you need as much information as possible in order to make well-informed decisions.

When people are given a sentence long enough to land them in prison, they are under DOC/BOP control from the moment they are sentenced.

Under applicable state laws or directives, DOC is responsible for calculating the length of stay (which can change based on new laws or interpretations of existing law, good or earned time, and whether sentences run consecutively or concurrently), and how the sentence is carried out. DOC policy, combined with relevant state or federal law, dictates every aspect of life inside. From criteria for custody levels, who goes to what institution, what type of programming is funded and eligibility criteria, how money and property are handled, medical and dental treatment, visitation and communication, clothing and hygiene, to what types of products are available for purchase; every aspect of life is controlled. This matters because while students are in your classroom, you are responsible for exercising that control, whether you are aware of what you are doing or not.

Most prison operations have similar structures and include a version of each of these areas: Custody (in the prison itself), Medical, Programming, Administrative, and a Community arm (outside the prison) that oversees parole and probation (they may have different names). There are several other departments but these are the ones you will interact with or hear from most often. I mention the Community aspect for educators who may be working in reentry, or who are trying to help students transition back to the community—you may interact with security staff in that department.

The elements that will most frequently impact your daily work are

- Custody: law enforcement/security inside the prison or jail
- Environment: requirements of the physical space and institution

- Medical: in charge of all medical and health-related needs or issues
- Programming: includes employment or "work programs," Education, vocational training and entrepreneurial initiatives, Treatment (drug/alcohol and sometimes for sex-related offenses), Parenting and other life skills, Corrections/Prison counselors, Volunteer programs, and Religion and Faith practice

Please bear in mind that I am writing about this from my experience as a teacher, which is a position at the bottom of the organization chart looking upward and sideways. My description of the organizational structure and roles is based on my daily interactions, not on a deep understanding of military hierarchy, security assignments, or overview of job descriptions.

Custody

Custody is security and considered of primary importance in any corrections environment. Most prison systems' missions include a public safety statement, where safety is primarily defined in in the context of physical confinement and social isolation. Anything you want to do in a carceral space needs the support of security staff—front-line guards, shift sergeants or lieutenants, or higher-level security personnel. Custody has the last word regarding anything that might be considered a "threat to security" and the definition of that phrase is as dependent on corrections culture and institutional practice as it is on policy and law.

Your Education department may have its own building, or it may just have use of a few rooms. Whatever the setup, you will have security staff assigned to your area, and they have the power to make your and your students' daily lives easy and smooth or very unpleasant. One of your priorities once you are hired and have gotten through your first days should be to meet with the Education security staff and start building your relationship with them. The more they trust you, the better your teaching life will be.

Environment

The primary focus of every carceral space is security. This translates into strict controls over almost every aspect of life for people living there, and (to a lesser degree) people who work there. If you are an experienced educator, working in this environment will be a major adjustment. Your work falls at the intersection of clashing bureaucracies and cultures, which will present ongoing challenges. If you are a program coordinator or manager, you may find yourself constantly winding through labyrinthian nightmares or into bureaucratic cul de sacs.

In this environment, treating everyone with true dignity and respect is a revolutionary act. Humanizing people in an environment designed to dehumanize and break their spirits is as important, if not more so, than offering a rigorous academic program. A combination of the two is the best possible approach, as either on its own is less impactful. It can be a grueling task to maintain high academic expectations that are mindful of the environment and flexible enough to accommodate circumstances beyond the control of your students. Creating learning spaces independent of the rigid demands of gatekeeper education that can flourish in carceral environments is necessary work but not easy.

A good friend of mine who has run programming inside for almost two decades always asks people how they respond to authority as part of the interview process. If you have never thought directly about your relationship to authority, think about it before you accept any job working in corrections, education or otherwise. Corrections is a hierarchical, top-down, para-military organization. Its focus is on security and it has a broad definition of what it considers threats to security. That definition includes the obvious (weapons, physical assault, escape) but also includes the less obvious (poor culture fits, challenges to authority, refusal to enforce discipline, and constant boundary pushing).

Whether you like it or not, if you want to work in a jail or prison, you will have to adapt your thinking to some degree and adopt a security perspective. Even if you personally don't agree, your ability to continue working with your students will depend on how well you can adapt to the environment. It is not an exaggeration to say that refusing to adapt and follow basic security protocols may put your students at great risk, so don't do it. If you don't think you can adapt, or don't want to, I strongly recommend you consider other ways you can work with or support system-impacted people.

Facility Entrance/Exits

Entering and exiting the facility usually involves three common security measures: Signing or checking you in/out, pulling or returning keys and/or a radio, and a security check. (Note: Volunteers will likely not pull keys)

When you enter a facility, your presence (name, date, reason for visit, time in/out) will be noted somewhere. You may scan a badge or sign a roster, but there should be a record of all that information for everyone who goes in. You may have to do this only at the main access point, or at every building you enter, it depends on the facility. This is used to make sure whoever went in comes back out. If you neglect to sign out, you will likely receive a call to confirm that you did leave the prison, and a warning about remembering to sign out. If you swipe or scan a badge, the same procedure applies.

If your work area is deep inside the facility or complex, you may have to pass through numerous gates and doors, as well as go through sally ports (a secure, controlled entryway). Making your way through the institution can take some time as security opens or closes doors depending on what other doors are open or closed when you request to be admitted. You will likely have to pass through at least one sally port, which can also take time if there are multiple people coming the other way, or if traffic jams up during a shift change.

If you are an employee or contractor, chances are that you will be assigned a set of keys. These keys are the property of the institution and must be checked out and returned every time you enter or leave your secure area. You may go through Public Access and pull keys, or you may be given your keyset by the officer at the access point. Some facilities have an automated key security system, which will log you taking and returning keys. Forgetting to check in your keys (and thus taking them home with you) will likely result in an angry phone call and trip to return them the first time. It is in your best interest to not let there be a second time.

Depending on the security at your institution or building, you may also have a key code, but code pads haven't replaced the need for keys in most places. Code pads may be used for access to certain parts of the facility, buildings, or parts of buildings, but keys are what get you into rooms. Key management is a big deal, both because of the security risk and the cost of replacing missing keys. Even a person with minimal access carries a keyset that would cost in the thousands to replace.

Keys are a major security issue, and you should have your keys on your body (in a pocket, clipped to a belt) whenever you are in the facility. Never leave them laying around and **do NOT take them off the premises**. Even more important, NEVER give your keys to a student or clerk, ask them to carry them or touch them in any way. Doing any of these things is a security risk for the institution, a potential job-losing risk for you, and could result in severe disciplinary measures for the incarcerated person, even if they were only doing what they were told.

Everyone who pulls keys has an assigned keyset and you only have keys for rooms you are approved to access. If you need keys for other rooms, you'll have to talk with your supervisor or, if you are the supervisor, with your liaison or the person in charge of keys. People in the same general work areas may pull the same sets of keys. If your department normally has people working a staggered schedule but an event, for example, means you are all there at the same time, you may end up not having enough keysets to go around. This is inconvenient but sometimes unavoidable.

Radios may or may not be required. There are two main types of radios, handheld and on the shoulder. If you get a radio, it will likely be handheld. Radios are like keys, i.e., keep them with you at all times and never let anyone but another staff member touch or use your assigned radio. Ask if you are going to be required to have a radio, and also make sure you will receive training on its use. There are definitely buttons you don't want to push and knobs you don't need to turn.

Facilities conduct security checks but when and how this is done is specific to the institution. Regular employees, volunteers, and visitors are all subject to different types of security checks, and may be subject to different requirements. Some facilities use body and x-ray scanners, random search generators, or require all bags and packages be manually cleared. Learn your facility's requirements as soon as possible and stick to them.

Badges

You will get some kind of identity badge based on whether you are agency staff, a contractor, or volunteer. Agency staff and contractors have similar levels of access and can move around their facility and work area freely, but volunteers must be escorted at all times. Everyone must have their badge visible at all times, wherever they are in the facility. Never take your badge off while you're in the facility and **never** allow a student or clerk to touch your badge.

Emergencies

Whether you are a volunteer or contractor, make sure you understand what is required of you during an emergency. Prisons are constructed so that what happens in one building may have little or no impact on other buildings. This often includes water, electrical, and HVAC, but older facilities may have more shared systems. Things happen all the time that won't impact you directly, although they may impact your students. If you are getting facility email, keep an eye out, although emergencies are not always shared via email.

Assuming you are an employee or contractor, you will get a significant chunk of training on emergency management during your onboarding (if you get any) and in yearly In-Service. The most important thing to know is who will be giving orders during emergency situations if your supervisor isn't around.

Clothing

Before your first day, make sure to ask your supervisor what clothing you are NOT allowed to wear. Prisons may ban certain colors or styles of clothing because they are "too similar" to what incarcerated people wear and are considered a security risk. Regardless of your gender, dress conservatively. Less skin is better, business casual with sleeves (3/4 or full), and modest neckline is usually a safe choice. My recommendation is no fragrance, minimal cosmetics and jewelry, but that is a personal choice based on facility requirements.

Your students may admire and compliment your clothing, shoes, hairstyle, and accessories. Your response depends on the situation, the institution's rules, and your boundaries. My general approach is that I don't make space in the conversation for sharing compliments, or commentary on appearance. If someone is persistent, I ignore the comment and return to the conversation at hand. There is no one script or approach that will work for everyone; we each have to enforce our own boundaries.

I do not recommend calling security or writing someone up for a mild comment, especially if it is their first misstep. It can be difficult to determine if someone has genuinely made a mistake, or if they are trying to get a response. I prefer to err on the side of giving people a first chance and offering a correction before taking a more drastic step. There are exceptions to this general rule, including 1) inappropriate comments (i.e., presumption of intimacy, physical objectification, ridicule, or aggression) and 2) when I have set an expectation for the group and someone tests the boundary, either publicly or privately. We will look at this more in the section on boundaries.

Parking

Most prisons I've visited have large parking lots that are a fair distance from my work area. You may have to park in the Visitor's spaces for a day or two before you are cleared for staff parking. Depending on how many gates, doors, and sally ports you have to clear, you will probably want to plan at least 30 minutes to get from your car to your work area for the first week or two. Keep this in mind for lunch and breaks, so you can plan your time. Prisons or jails in urban areas may be different but until you are familiar with the security routines and route to your work area, give yourself extra time. There are any number of slow-downs that can happen at access points, and you can be stuck waiting for a long time if security is handling emergencies.

Meals

There are rarely nearby food options, so you'll want to bring plenty of food and snacks unless you want to eat out of vending machines. You may have the option to get lunch from the chow hall, but I can't say I recommend the food. Make sure your utensils are not sharp edged, glass, or metal. I carried a plastic spork/spatula combo for years and it was perfect. I also kept a plastic reusable dish, bowl, and towel in my desk, along with a minor condiment stash and a couple of plastic water bottles. Prisons already have enormous carbon footprints so the less trash you can generate the better.

You may want to keep a small travel kit in your office, in case the prison locks down. Hygiene items, food and snacks, a water bottle, and washcloths or wipes would make an extended stay at the prison slightly more bearable. If the entire prison locks down and you're inside, you may be there until the lockdown lifts, or you're cleared to leave.

Training

Training varies depending on state, municipality, type of staff role, and whether you are an agency, contractor, or volunteer. You may or may not receive new employee training, especially if you are not agency staff or security.

If you are a contractor (even if you don't get training when you start) or agency staff, you will be required to go through yearly training "refreshers" usually called In Service. In Service has a number of staple courses, although this can differ across facilities and may be different in BOP. Courses will likely include Emergency/First Aid certification, fire extinguishers, weather-related (e.g., extreme heat or cold) safety, Internet and network precautions, Emergency Management Systems (EMS), which includes at least an overview of incident response, bloodborne pathogens, and occasionally a "soft" skill like communication or de-escalation.

You will also have numerous classes on the Prison Rape Elimination Act (PREA). PREA is a federal law passed in 2003 in an attempt to eliminate rape inside prisons, jails, and other lockup facilities (Department of Justice, Office of Justice Programs, n.d.). In 2012, the Department of Justice (DOJ) published the final PREA standards in the National Registry, and carceral spaces have been working on compliance ever since (National PREA Resource Center, n.d.;United States Department of Justice, 2012). The DOJ Inspector General, in a special report, stated that

> It is important to note that consent is never a legal defense for corrections staff who engage in sexual acts with inmates. According to federal law, all sexual relations between staff and inmates are considered abuse. Even if a sexual act would have been considered consensual if it occurred outside of a prison, by statute it is criminal sexual abuse when it occurs inside a prison…. As a result, staff sexual relations with inmates is always illegal. (Office of the Inspector General, 2005)

PREA, the law and standards, goes to the heart of a crucial element of prison life—the inability to say "no," or withdraw consent. Consent matters, in part, because people can withdraw that consent. The consequences of saying "no" in prison can be dire, and potentially life-threatening, especially if they are saying "no" to the people in charge of their well-being. Whether you are agency staff, contractor, volunteer, or any other person in the prison but not incarcerated, you cannot have consensual sex with an incarcerated person. PREA also applies this definition to sex between incarcerated people, which is prohibited for the same reason—there can be no absolute certainty of consent.

When you work in a prison, you are an authority figure, even if you don't think of yourself in that manner. Whether you choose to exercise that power or not, incarcerated people are required to obey you when you give directives, and the Dominator dynamic influences every interaction. This mix of toxic power dynamics and the inability to give and withdraw consent means that outside of a strict and narrow definition, relationships between staff and incarcerated people are suspect. Your training may also include setting and maintaining boundaries, with an emphasis on using the code of conduct and facility rules to enforce those boundaries.

This section is fairly short by design, as there is no way to know what kind of training you will receive. Whatever you do receive, it is unlikely to include a straightforward discussion of corrections culture, or its hostility toward education and learning—especially for incarcerated people. When I started at the prison, there was no agency-sponsored training and I had to learn on the job from my colleagues and supervisor. Trying to map what I knew about education to working in the facility was confusing and disorienting, and I spent a long time not understanding why things weren't getting done, or why agency staff viewed me with suspicion.

Ultimately, that lack of understanding, combined with burnout, initiated my departure from that position. My hope is that you will have a better overall experience, thus giving your students a better education.

Medical

The Medical department wields enormous influence over daily schedules. All medical care is strictly controlled, from dispensing medication to seeing people with cold symptoms, to scheduling medical procedures. Life-threatening emergencies aside, visits to Medical are scheduled and the patient (your student) may or may not know about a scheduled visit until the day of. People may see that they are on the callout and not know why, and they rarely know in advance. When someone is on a Medical callout, it is imperative that they go to that callout as getting procedures and visits with specialists scheduled can take weeks if not months.

Staff Roles

Job titles in a bureaucracy are unhelpful. Job titles can hint at a person's job duties, but even that is inconsistent across departments. This isn't different than other places of employment, but when you are trying to navigate an institution as siloed as corrections, knowing who to contact for what is an enormous time-saver. This knowledge may also save you from mistakes that can get you into more trouble than it would in other places. Get a copy of the organization chart for your facility and familiarize yourself with the different departments, especially the administrative support personnel. They're the people who can likely answer questions about how to get things done. If you are part of an education team, talk to your dean or your department's administrative personnel first.

The exception is security rankings, which mirror the military hierarchy, and at least let you know where people are in the food chain. Through the rest of this text, I'll refer to staff by role, rather than job title (which differ across facilities, unions, and jurisdictions), and have split these into security and non-security. I am listing only the roles you might interact with regularly, and not all facilities will have all of these roles.

Common Non-Security Roles

Corrections counselors: this role is in place to help incarcerated people navigate the corrections bureaucracy. They are often former security staff and may or may not have training or experience as a counselor or social worker. Knowing who your students' counselors are is helpful, and having a positive relationship with counseling staff is ideal. Counselors are one source of referrals to education programming and are considered the go-to or first point of contact for most non-disciplinary questions and issues. They know the prison system and can be a resource when you are trying to understand how particular processes work.

A disinterested or hostile counselor is a serious roadblock. Counselors can stay in their positions for a long time and they are permission and referral gatekeepers for their caseload. Encroaching on decisions a counselor considers their territory is a risk, as is questioning those decisions. Trying to go around a hostile counselor, even if permitted, can have repercussions for you and your student, so be certain you have explored all your options and your supervisor is involved.

Callout management/coordination: This is an administrative position and helpful to know in case you have questions about your callouts, or scheduling mishaps. Callouts are likely run and printed at least twice a day and may be done just before each shift. There is usually a person assigned to deal with all the logistics, run and print, and make sure the sheets are delivered to units/dorms and staff. If students are suddenly not showing up or telling you they are scheduled elsewhere, checking with the callout coordinator is a good starting point.

Facility access (different than Public Access): There is someone assigned to do background checks and paperwork for daily (or one-time) visitors, which is a different visitor designation than regular volunteers. If you are part of an Education department, check with your administrative staff, as they may assist with getting clearance for a daily visitor. What's important to know is that you cannot bring in visitors (or volunteers) without prior clearance and approval. If you are bringing in a high-profile visitor (an elected official, for example), you may also need to get approval from the public information or communications staff.

Your supervisor. I'm including this role on the list because who you report to differs on how education is handled at each facility. You may report to a college dean or director, a Volunteer program coordinator, corrections staff acting in the role of dean or director, or any number of other people. During your interview, clarify who you will directly report to and how your department fits into the facility's structure.

Volunteer coordinator. The volunteer coordinator is responsible for all volunteer programs. Most programs that don't have a formalized agreement or contract for services with the facility fall under the purview of Volunteer programs. Common examples are AA, NA, movement programs such as Yoga Behind Bars, faith-based activities, arts, crafts, writing groups, Toastmasters, nonviolent communication, and education. Education can be both formal (i.e., you are a contractor and have many of the same access and privileges of staff) and volunteer programming (you are a volunteer and do not have the same access and privileges as staff), depending on a variety of factors.

If you are considered regular or contract staff, you will interact with the volunteer co-ordinator only as needed for your program or class. If you are a volunteer, you or your supervisor will work with them regularly. Volunteers almost always have to be escorted everywhere (including the bathroom). Staff may be required to remain with you while you are conducting classes, or you may be allowed to conduct class but not leave the classroom unescorted. If you are a volunteer, make SURE you understand exactly what you are and are not allowed to do, and where you are allowed to be in the facility. Volunteer programs have precarious access at best and mistakes can result in grave consequences.

Staff in Charge of Badges, Background Checks, and Room Scheduling

If you are a volunteer, the Volunteer coordinator will hopefully take care of all of these for you. If you are part of a department, your dean or administrative folks are your point people. What is helpful is just to know that these are all separate tasks and in an emergency, there are specific people you can call with questions. Even if your role is as an instructor only, you will find that knowing who to call if a visitor needs a badge, or if a background check hasn't come through, or your scheduled room has people in it can save your plans.

Medical

You will likely have little access to medical staff, unless you run into them in a hallway. Medical areas are quite secure and you won't wander into the Medical area by accident. Medical information is supposed to be kept confidential, and prisons are bound by HIPPA regulations, as well as whatever security policies and procedures the facility has in place. If something comes up around a student's health, I do not recommend attempting to contact medical staff with questions. Your best option is to check in with the student's counselor. They will not give you medical information, but may be able to tell you when the student will be back in class, or help you get materials to a student, if possible.

Program Manager

"Programming" is a very broad term that influences almost all aspects of daily prison life other than meals, medical, and security. Depending on how your institution is set up, programming may be handled primarily from one umbrella department, or might be scattered throughout various areas. Regardless, there will likely be one person who oversees most of the programming (we'll call them the Corrections Programming Manager, or CPM) and you should know who they are. If you are a teacher or administrative support, you may not interact with this person directly, but your supervisor probably will.

The CPM is a decision-maker when it comes to implementing anything new, and may have to be consulted for event planning, guests, or anything outside of your normal teaching routine. They may also have influence over other corrections staff who can refer students to Education, encouraging them to make more referrals, work with students' Education schedules, and smooth the way with security. They are gatekeepers, whatever their titles, and understanding how they operate will help you better shape your ideas and requests.

Work/Employment Coordinator

I ran a work-based education program that was considered "work" and students were paid to be in the program. This was true of several of the Education programs in that prison, although not of ABE/GED®. I have learned that this is, by far, the exception—most education programs and classes have to accommodate work schedules and employment is almost always prioritized over Education. This seems surprising, given that there is so much research demonstrating the importance of education, but a closer look behind the curtain of prison employment offers some understanding.

Almost all adult carceral facilities use incarcerated people as part of their work force. Thanks to the 13th Amendment of the United States Constitution, it is legal to use incarcerated people as a slave labor force. Prisons and jails take advantage of that legal opportunity by requiring employment or "work programming" from the incarcerated population. Jurisdictions approach this differently, with some states paying people, others mandating that all incarcerated adults must work without pay, and jails all operating independently.

While it is true that many people could benefit from workforce development efforts and job skills training, these outcomes are not always at the core of prison or jail employment. Most "work" positions in carceral spaces require minimal skill, talent, and engagement. While there is nothing wrong with taking pride in one's work, no matter what that work may be, you will see that your students' minds and talents are often ignored and wasted in the work they can get. There are exceptions to this, but eligibility for specialized positions can exclude large numbers of people. Much of the work is janitorial, groundskeeping and maintenance, road cleanup crews, laundry, and food service. In many Western states, incarcerated people fight fires, although most states do not allow them to continue that work as paid firefighters upon release.

There are a small number of specialized positions as clerks or program assistants. These positions often pay on the higher end of the pay scale and are sought after. Many are in programs, and Education departments often have clerks and tutors helping with ABE/GED ® classes, with other tutors assigned to programs they've completed. The students who completed my program were in high demand as clerks because they had solid computer and administrative skills.

There are a number of reasons why prison employment is problematic. Security staff would argue that incarcerated people are too big a security risk for most positions, especially positions that require contact with anyone beyond who they would normally encounter in their daily routines. Incarcerated people are also subject to abrupt shifts in circumstance including reassignment to new living quarters, transfer to another facility, or disciplinary procedures. This uncertainty influences hiring processes as "employers" do not want high turnover in positions that require a lot of training.

But practical considerations aside, let's take a look at the combination of legalized slavery and mythos of "rehabilitation" used to build a complex house of economic cards.

Prisons themselves are dependent on cheap/slave labor to fulfill their need for low or no-skill labor necessary for day-to-day functions. This reduces the need to hire permanent state or municipal employees into these positions, which can be framed as cost savings for states and counties.

Thanks to legislative efforts in the 1970s that were indefinitely continued in the 1990s (Penal labor in the United States, n.d.), prison-made goods can cross state lines and people making those goods can earn higher wages than other incarcerated people doing the daily scut work of the prison. Many states (and the Federal BOP) have created for-profit arms of their DOCs, with jobs in those for-profit industries paying more than standard prison jobs, but far less than non-incarcerated people would demand, and with no benefits, retirement, or representation.

Some states have passed legislation requiring that contracts for certain types of goods (office furniture, for example) must be given to the for-profit prison industries, or that bids from the for-profit arm of the state DOC must be prioritized. Federal Prison Industries (FPI), the for-profit arm of the BOP, and housed in the Department of Justice (DOJ) enjoys similar benefits and privileges with regard to contracts.

Other state agencies may contract with the for-profit arm of DOC for cheap/slave labor to provide certain services, such as staffing call centers, producing license plates, food preparation, and laundry management for a wide range of entities. These services may be separate from the same services used by the prison, or not (i.e., there is an in-house laundry service for the prison, and a separate, for-profit laundry service for outside agencies).

The Work Opportunity Tax Credit (WOTC), which provides a $2,400/year tax credit to agencies who hire people with conviction histories, is used by employers while people are still in custody at work releases or halfway houses. Whether those same people are retained in those jobs after they are fully released is unclear. Although WOTC itself is an incentive for employers and intended to encourage hiring, it may have become a way to reward employers for taking people into short-term, entry-level, low or no-skill positions that ultimately give them little advantage in the labor market.

This may seem like a lot of background information just to talk about a staff role, but I am trying to clarify an aspect of corrections that is confusing and often invisible—why employment/work programs that are overseen by DOC may refuse to cooperate or accommodate Education programs. When you find yourself frustrated by the inflexible demands of prison employment, remember that you are up against enormous economic forces and the systems that have created them. Prison labor has become critical to both the US economy and the prison-industrial complex and reducing recidivism, workforce development, or increasing employability are no longer its main incentives.

Even with all of those underlying pieces, it is always worth building a good relationship with the Work/Employment Coordinator. Keep your expectations low and always have a backup plan for students who aren't available for important classroom events. This relationship is also helpful in finding your students a position that may benefit them after they leave your program or classroom.

Common Security Roles

This is an area I am less familiar with as I have not worked in security, so you should check with your facility to see how these roles and duties are assigned. I have avoided assigning responsibilities or duties to a specific ranking.

Public Access

There is a Public Access (PA) point at every carceral facility and you will likely go through this access point whenever you go to work. PA may be inside or outside a secure perimeter, but every compound will have a main point of entry, even if portions of the compound have a separate access area. For example, if you work at a compound that has a Minimum security facility co-located with a Medium/Maximum facility, the PA for the entire compound may be at the Medium/Maximum facility, with a smaller access point at the Minimum facility.

These points are all going to be constructed and managed differently, but they all control the flow of people into and out of the compound. This means they

- make sure everyone who goes in is who they say they are and has a documented reason for going in,
- make sure that everyone leaving is who they say they are,
- check that no contraband goes in or out, and
- confirm that everyone who goes in actually leaves.

They have other duties but these are the four that will impact you most directly. PA is staffed by security, although there may be administrative and management offices in the same area. It is important that you understand the policies and procedures that dictate access, especially if you plan on bringing in outside guests or volunteers. Maintaining a professional, cordial relationship with the staff at PA is in your best interest, as is following PA policy and procedure at all times.

Building Security

Every building in the facility has assigned security personnel. If Education is in its own building, it will likely have one or two officers assigned during the day and possibly through the swing shift. Evening security may be more sparse meaning less people or less presence in your building. If you teach in the evenings, make sure you know your building security and their routines. Check in with them when you come in, at least once during the evening, and when you leave.

Unit Staff

Everyone living in a prison has an assigned living space; cells or dorm-style are most common. These are physically grouped into tiers, blocks, units or some other designation (I'll use units from here on), and the units are part of a building or wing of a building. People are generally not allowed to visit between units, and every unit has security staff assigned, and may also have a corrections counselor. I hesitate to go into further detail because this is one of those areas where prisons and jails vary so widely it's hard to know what would be useful and not confusing.

If possible, learn the name of the main unit officer and the unit counselor. It is likely there are several officers who work on a single unit, but if there is probably only one assigned counselor. There may be a "case bank" counselor who handles a large caseload of people considered to be "low need."

Unit officers have significant control over your students' daily lives, in ways people who have not been incarcerated cannot understand. As you build your relationship with your students and learn about the prison and DOC staff, you will be better able to glean context from what students say. While students may not share details of their lives outside the classroom, know that much of what happens in their lives is outside of their control. At the least, speak with your colleagues about how they handle student behavior, and what information they try to uncover before making decisions. Note: Be cautious when talking with students about their interactions with security. This type of conversation can be easily misinterpreted as allowing a student to triangulate staff, or you questioning security's decisions.

Shift Sergeants and Lieutenants

Every shift (including the swing shift) has a designated Sergeant and Lieutenant. Depending on your role, you may not interact with them much, but you should at least know who they are in case you need to speak with them. I found them most helpful when planning security for an event, considering certain kinds of disciplinary action, and if I needed to change something about my class time or location that would impact security. If you are working in an Educational department, your dean or one of your administrative coordinators may be your point people for these tasks.

Master Control

Master Control (or whatever name it is called where you work) is the security hub for the entire facility. If you have two facilities on the compound (ex: Medium and Minimum located within walking, or short driving, distance), Master Control will probably be in the more security facility. All communication (phone and radio) is handled by them, and they are responsible for all facility security at all times. It is highly unlikely you will interact with or visit Master Control but, depending on how things are handled at your facility, emergency calls may be routed to them.

Shifts and Building Assignments

Security staff are usually on a shift schedule, although security administrative staff (i.e., wardens, superintendents, associate superintendents, etc.) may be on a more typical office schedule. A shift schedule might be: 6:00 a.m.–2:00 p.m., 2:00 p.m.–10:00 p.m., 10:00 p.m.–6:00 a.m. with "swing" staff from 2:00–6:00 or so. The time around shift change is busy, especially first shift as there may be office workers coming in around that time.

Security staff can move around depending on daily needs, and scheduled reassignments happen once or twice a year. Changes in building personnel can directly impact your daily work life, but there is nothing you can do to influence this process. Make the effort to learn the names and faces of security assigned to your building or area, and know that those assignments can change at any time. The most common scenario is that you will have one shift change during your daily work schedule, although coming in early or staying late means you may see two. Take the time to learn the shift schedule for your facility and, if possible, make sure you know the shift Sergeants and Lieutenants.

Do not routinely depend on personal relationships or favors. If the only way you can get something done is because a certain person is on duty, reconsider what you need. This type of situation is guaranteed to come to light and, at best, will be regarded unfavorably. At worst, you and/or the person doing you favors could find yourselves in trouble.

Programs

Programs are the rehabilitative arm of corrections. The word itself is an umbrella term that covers many activities not directly related to security or daily living. Programs are run by agency staff (e.g., DOC, BOP), contractors (e.g., colleges, mental health providers), and volunteers and there will be an agency staff person responsible for overseeing programming. Volunteers may or may not fall under the general Programming umbrella, but volunteer programs do have to coordinate to use the same space and resources.

People may participate voluntarily, be required by DOC, or have to complete a certain type of program as part of their sentence. Completing a specific course of treatment is often required, and can include programs for substance use, sex offenses, or cognitive behavioral issues. Even if a program is not required by a judge, a counselor can make a referral if they consider it beneficial to the person's stated long-term goals. In some states, people without a high school credential may be required by state law to work on getting that credential. High school credentialing programs (most often the for-profit GED®) are one of the more consistent education-related offerings across correctional facilities.

Programs may be handled through agency contracts, non-profit organizations, or volunteer groups. Of those three, agency contracts are usually the only interaction that have a financial component. Agency contracts may be handled at the level of jurisdiction (i.e., state or county), or an individual facility may coordinate with a volunteer or non-profit organization.

For example, a state DOC might contract with that state's higher education board to provide college programming in all state facilities, where county jail might contract with the college in one county (or region) to provide classes. Volunteer programs are usually dependent on individual facilities for access so a volunteer-run program at Prison A may not be available at Prison B, even if they are both state prisons. Many Education programs are run as Volunteer programs, with costs covered by a combination of student financial aid and outside funding.

Eligibility for a particular program is not a given for all incarcerated people. In the states where I've worked, corrections agencies are responsible for administering sentencing, which includes (among other things) calculating the length of sentence, whether it will run consecutively or concurrently, and level of custody. Any or all of these calculations can impact whether someone is considered eligible for certain types of programs, and those eligibility criteria are determined by the agency. The agency also decides where people will be incarcerated, and when and why they will be moved. You may think this aspect of corrections is removed from your day-to-day work, but it is closer than it appears.

Program eligibility criteria can include current and past behavior and discipline, length of sentence, custody level, counselor referral or approval, and may require a GED®. DOC eligibility criteria does not always mesh well with release timing and program availability, so people do not always get into court-ordered programming until they are very close to release. Unfortunately, education is rarely court-ordered, so people can be pulled out of Educational programming to fulfill court-ordered programming as deemed necessary. Facility transfers, changes in custody level, behavior, and discipline can all impact eligibility and participation in education, and your class (or program) will take second place to security decisions.

Agency-sponsored education (which is paid for, in part, by state tax dollars) is not available to all incarcerated people. There are logistical reasons for this (such as limited educational offerings in remote prisons), but eligibility criteria are a major factor. Some types of eligibility may be determined by state law. For example, a person with a life sentence, or life without parole, may have limited access to certain types of programs, especially those that are considered rehabilitative and are prioritized for people returning to the community. That person may be able to take education classes but only if they pay and if there is an empty seat.

People who receive long sentences may not be eligible for any programming until they are a certain number of years from release (or "to the gate"). So a person with a 20-year sentence could spend the first 13–15 years denied access to agency-sponsored programs like Education and Treatment, although they may be able to participate in Volunteer programs.

Despite how removed most of this is from your classroom, decisions you make about discipline and grading can have bigger impacts than you realize. You will be expected to follow your facility's disciplinary requirements but in most cases, you get to choose the level of discipline you think is needed. Before you make those decisions, talk with your supervisor and, if possible, the student's corrections counselor, and be sure you understand the consequences for the student.

Education Logistics

Education is most often part of programming in longer-term facilities, although there is a strong push for getting more opportunity into jails, as they are where the majority of people are locked up. As already mentioned, Education can be part of structured funding (i.e., agency-wide contracts with a college or colleges), or may be offered by volunteer programs, or through alternative funding sources. Agency-funded educational programs often require that participants earn a credential, which can be a degree, certificate, or professional certification.

Education logistics are a constant tangle of funding, space and resource limitations, lack of technology, constraints on state funds, and staff availability. Education offerings (both quantity and quality) vary greatly from state to state and facility to facility and there may or may not be oversight outside of the corrections agency to provide consistency. Without strong support from someone in the corrections agency itself, the outlook for students is bleak, especially when cultures and bureaucracies clash.

There is a constant tug-of-war between programs for access to incarcerated people, all of it happening within the framework of security. What differentiates Education from other programs is that not all colleges have the same offerings (the GED® is an exception). Mental/behavioral health providers all work from a standard program or curriculum, as defined in their contract with the agency. This curriculum is standardized, no matter where it is delivered or who delivers it, so people are getting the same information, delivered in the same progression. They may have to repeat work or catch up, but they move from facility to facility and meet the desired outcome.

This is not the case with college-level education programs. Colleges all operate independently and while they may all offer a two- or four-year degree with the same name, there is minimal standardization of content. Education programs are location-dependent, meaning they offer only what their local college offers, so moving people from facility to facility can create problems in terms of learning, incomplete degrees and credentials, lost funding dollars, and post-prison education planning. Offering secured Internet or other distance learning options is one solution to this problem, but is not in the near future for most facilities.

People who oversee Education programming have to take all of these barriers into account as they design curriculum, lesson plans, and courses of study, and it is a difficult task. Students do not have control over where they live, and their wishes around education are not the priority when security is making decisions. Even in states or regions where colleges agree to coordinate their educational offerings, students may find themselves with unnecessary credits, or having to decide between a program they aren't interested in, consequences of refusing an unwanted program, or no education at all. The exception to the "non-standard" education is the (for-profit) GED®.

The (for-Profit) GED®

In corrections, the most prevalent education-related measurements is the for-profit GED®. I refer to it in that manner for both accuracy and as a reminder. Taxpayers are paying for K–12 public education (which is failing these students) and then later, in prisons, where people are forced to sit with packets and take tests that have little or no connection to learning, or even contain useful educational content.

Before readers jump up to defend instructors or the presence of the for-profit GED® in prisons, remember that this isn't about whether instructors are doing a good job, or the need for education and learning opportunities for incarcerated people. I have worked with instructors who had rooms of materials and created individualized curricula for every student to ensure that they were learning, not just memorizing packets. I have also worked with instructors who did nothing but sit in a room while people struggled.

According to the Prison Policy Initiative,

- "More than half of formerly incarcerated people hold only a high school diploma or GED® — credentials which have diminishing value in today's job market.
- Unlike the general public, people who have been to prison are more likely to have a GED® than they are to have traditional high school diplomas. And three-quarters of those GED® certificates are earned in prison" (Couloute, 2018).

Though there are studies and data that demonstrate that completing a GED® while incarcerated has an impact on rates of recidivism, there is scant information on whether that credential increases people's well-being, quality of life, or even leads to living-wage employment. What we do know is that close to 60% of incarcerated (and formerly incarcerated) people's traditional high school education was cut short (Couloute, 2018) and that the GED®, once an alternative high school credential, has become less of an alternative and more the norm for incarcerated students.

Prior to its sale to a for-profit entity, the GED® was classroom-based, teacher-led instruction. Students took the same set of tests and received the same credential, but classes and curricula varied, even as they prepared students for those tests. Even with teacher-led instruction, this was a less than ideal situation as, with any standardized testing, instruction can focus more on test-taking than actual learning.

Privatization of the GED® when for-profit Pearson VUE took over its administration in 2014 meant increased testing costs, as well as costs for technology to administer the now computer-only exam. This may have resulted in less funding for instructors and classroom teaching needs, but there is no easily available information on those numbers. According to the Connecticut Mirror, the number of people passing the test dropped by close to 90% (from 781 to 68) in 2015–2016, then increased to 165 in 2016–2017 (Kara, 2017). Whether these data are still accurate is uncertain, as finding comparisons from before and after privatization is difficult (Strauss, 2015; Mendez, 2017; Vyse, 2012).

In prisons today, these classes are often conducted as "self-study" which means students are given packets, with minimal classroom instruction, and assistance with the tasks of learning. This is not necessarily the choice of the instructor, but with limited funding and headcounts to meet, classrooms have become production lines. People who have successfully completed their credential are often recruited to work as Teaching Assistants, and provide both academic and personal support for students trying to learn enough to pass the four standardized tests.

As an educator who has seen the variety of ways the current, for-profit GED® is taught and administered, I am hard-pressed to consider it useful beyond a marker of completion. I don't deny that completing the credential is an incredible accomplishment for many students and that finishing a difficult endeavor has a positive impact on their self-confidence and esteem.

I do not, however, believe that students, especially adult students, gain much from the experience that increases their capacity for or interest in learning. Even with increased self-confidence and pride, the structure of the for-profit GED® (self-paced packets, limited classroom instruction and student interaction) contains almost none of the rich engagement necessary to stoke curiosity and love of learning. The result is students who can pass the required tests, but are ill-quipped to succeed in college-level classrooms.

Our ethics and values as educators demand that we continually challenge why we keep administering a test we know is nothing but a checkbox, one that has decreased in value in increasingly competitive employment markets. The for-profit GED® is also a perfect example of prioritizing one framework of knowledge over every other. We have reduced the meaningful learning students should get during their formative years to a collection of paper packets (or online modules) devoid of meaning or connection to their lived experience. And while I believe that student success in accomplishing any goal should never be diminished, our students deserve better.

Vocational Training

My experience as a corrections educator was with community college programming. Community colleges are often the main partners for state DOCs in bringing education inside both youth and adult facilities. Some DOCs will manage their own educational programming, which means education staff are corrections employees and may not have access to faculty training and professional development offered by colleges.

Vocational and technical programs are a solid go-to for programming as state lawmakers can easily connect the dots to employment, coming back around to the (education + employment = lower recidivism = greater public safety) equation. Some states will offer vocational programs but not degrees, even if the educational content is identical to that offered on college campuses. Even in states where educational programming is supported, availability is vastly overwhelmed by need, corrections culture, space limitations, and policies that tightly control access, and not all prisons have equal opportunity to offer high-demand programs.

College Degrees

Four-year university degrees are even more scarce than two-year programs, and likely paid for entirely through private donors, foundations, and other funding streams. Organizations like University Beyond Bars and Mt. Tamalpais College (formerly the Prison University Project) work to offer advanced degrees in prisons where they have access, but are highly localized. Groups like the Black Prisoner's Caucus may partner with local colleges for operational and/or academic support for their peer teaching programs.

Until recently, Pell grant funds were available only to prisons who had applied for and received permission to access these funds through the Second Chance Pell program originally launched during the Obama administration (International Corrections & Prisons Association, n.d.), expanded in early 2020 (Vera Institute of Justice, 2020), and then re-opened to all incarcerated people in late 2020 (Cantora, 2020). Pell funding for correspondence learning has technical requirements that present challenges in corrections environments, but wider access to funding may incentivize colleges to propose solutions.

Without Pell funding, the majority of advanced degrees attained through correspondence courses can run upward of $500 out-of-pocket per class. While $500 may not seem like much in terms of per-credit cost, keep in mind that incarcerated people are paid pennies an hour, if they are paid at all. If an incarcerated person doesn't have money already, or people outside who have financial means, saving enough money to pay for even one class is an enormous hurdle.

Other Options

Faith-based initiatives are often combined with a cognitive change element, faith study, and an education element. Volunteers and non-profits will may run programs such as bee-keeping, construction and trades pre-apprenticeship classes, master gardeners and gardening, dog-training, small business development, and short-term, industry-specific classes. Regardless of popularity, these programs are often on precarious footing as funding is inconsistent, and DOC can choose to terminate a program without consequence or explanation.

Gender and Sexuality

The body of research on women in prison has begun expanding in the last few years but we still have relatively little information on how gender impacts the experience of incarceration. As in many fields, the default research subjects have been men, with minimal distinction in the final reporting on race, ethnicity, sexual orientation, religious preferences, or even age. My experience working in a women's prison, reading and speaking with incarcerated and formerly incarcerated scholars, and work in reentry informs most of my thinking around this topic, so I recommend additional study to increase your understanding of gender responsive best practices.

Gender and sexuality are charged topics in any carceral space, and are often lumped into admonishments about the dangers of manipulation and warnings to refrain from sexual relationships with incarcerated people. While discussions of manipulation and sexual relationships must happen, it is harmful and discriminatory to consider them only in the broader conversation about gender and sexuality, especially as those topics are reserved almost exclusively for working with women.

Public, high-level conversations about gender responsivity, until the last three years, have been rare. At best, they more often happened at the front-line worker level only. Women and LGBTQIA people continue to suffer additional harm from institutions that have shown minimal interest in adapting to their needs. Creating a trauma-responsive space, when there is such a dearth of gender and sexuality-specific information in the fields of both trauma and incarceration presents a number of challenges, especially with regard to relationships and community building.

First Day Checklist

Your first days on the job will be a whirlwind of paperwork, pictures, and getting in and out of the facility. Don't expect to remember much, but take notes (especially names) and ask for clarification later. You may be required to attend an orientation, or not; it depends on what training is offered and to whom. I was contract staff and, as I've already mentioned, the prison offered no orientation or new employee training for contract staff. The prisons I worked with most recently required a week-long orientation for all staff, including contract staff, and a six-week intensive boot camp for anyone working over 30 hours in a facility.

Remember, the learning curve is steep so expect that you will need things explained multiple times. They still may not make sense until you have to do them, or they happen, so ask a lot of questions. Hopefully either your supervisor or your prison liaison will have a checklist but in case they don't, I've put one together for you.

Entering the Facility

What is the sign-in procedure for Public Access? For your building?

Have you checked your bags to make sure you aren't bringing in inappropriate items (e.g., anything made out of metal or glass, any kind of knife or scissors)?

Did you pack some snacks and bring a water bottle?

Where is your work area? What is the building designation? Which room or area is your work area? Where is it located in the facility? Do you know how to get there?

You may not be allowed to bring in personal ID or credit cards, so leave them in the car if you are uncertain.

Are you dressed appropriately? Check with your supervisor or prison liaison in advance to find out if there are any types or colors of clothing that staff should not wear. More conservative is better in the beginning. If you are uncertain about an item of clothing, bring something different so you won't have to go all the way home to change (yes, this will probably happen at least once).

Bring a layer or two of clothing and plan to leave a sweater or top layer at work. Room temperatures can fluctuate during the day, especially if your room faces the afternoon sun.

Badge and Security

Who is escorting you until you get your own badge? What time do they come to work and where are you meeting them? Volunteer—who is escorting you? What time and where are you meeting them?

Will you be pulling keys? A radio? If it will take a few days for you to be cleared and trained, who will help with keys in the meantime? Will you have a co-worker nearby with a radio?

If you have an emergency with no staff or radio around, what is the procedure? In some facilities, you can knock the phone off its cradle; in others there is a number you can dial. 911 may be directed to Master Control, so don't dial that number unless you are told to do so.

Technology

Did you leave your phone, camera, or any other electronics in your car?

Make sure you don't have any USB drives, CDs, or other storage media in your bags or supplies.

Personnel

Who are the building officers during your workday?

Who is handling your technology access?

If your department or program has administrative or coordinator support, who are they? Where are they located?

Who is a go-to person for general questions?

Logistics

Where are the bathrooms?

What is the emergency number?

Where is your phone?

What is the Help desk number?

The Teaching Space

In many ways, teaching in carceral spaces is like teaching anywhere else. You'll have students you do and don't like, who do and don't like you, who are brilliant and lazy and annoying and heartwarming. With all these similarities, there is a caveat: You can never forget that you are not teaching in a free space. You are responsible for remembering where you are and the constraints you are under **at all times**. Forgetting these two things can put you at risk and, perhaps more importantly, can put your students at risk. Never forget that while you get to leave at the end of the day, they cannot. Things that seem inconsequential to you may have serious repercussions for them.

Prisons are designed to intimidate and reinforce who has power and who doesn't, and adapting to teaching inside is different for everyone. Teachers who are in the facility a few hours a week have a shorter learning curve and less interaction with the corrections system. Teachers who are in the facility 30+ hours a week have a much steeper curve that includes adjusting to an environment that doesn't always welcome education.

Statistically, over 50% of your students did not finish high school. If you are teaching college-level coursework, they may have a GED® that they got in prison or in youth detention. Your students will be all ages and levels of learning ability, some may not have been in a classroom in decades. Reviewing instructional tools and the basics of how to learn up front helps reduce shame and frustration for everyone.

50%+ of your students may have a diagnosed or undiagnosed learning disability, some other type of disability or a traumatic brain injury. Most jails and prisons do not offer special education teachers or the testing necessary for people to receive legal accommodations through the ADA. Make sure you know who is responsible for ADA requests for accommodations: your educational organization or the corrections facility. If it is the corrections facility, you may need to work out some "soft" accommodations to help the student while their request makes its way through the bureaucracy.

Your free campus teaching tools may be limited, or difficult to access. Start treating technology and any non-standard tools as condiments—nice to have but not strictly necessary. If you can find ways to bring them in consistently, that's excellent but be prepared to teach without them. If your teaching relies on technology, your coordinator or supervisor should work that out in advance, but I always advise having some back-pocket non-technology projects for when things go awry.

Prisons are places of power extremes and your classroom is no exception. People adopt behaviors that benefit them and keep them safe, and you will see a broad range of adaptive behaviors. Regardless of the behavior, or how you might perceive or label individual students, your responses and behavior **must** remain the same—calm and measured. It is not an exaggeration to say that a calm, measured, and consistent approach to people and situations can be the difference between success or failure in corrections education.

You will make mistakes. We have all made mistakes. Some will turn out okay but some may not, and there may be nothing you can do change the outcome. The best action to take once you recognize you've made a mistake is to immediately notify the appropriate people. Be honest, even if you are embarrassed or angry, and do not try to excuse your decision. It helps if you can give a clear description of why you made that particular mistake, although you may still get the same outcome. Remember that prisons are reactionary spaces, and those reactions are usually framed by rigid codes of rules and conduct, and maintain your calm, measured approach.

Physical Setup and Property

Prison classrooms are not standard, even across the same facility. Some will be equipped with smartboards and projectors, others with chairs, a table, and whiteboard. If you are part of an agency program, you will hopefully have a room more like what you would have on a college campus. You will have some freedom in your classroom, but hold off on rearranging the furniture your first day. When I first walked into my classroom, I wanted to change the layout into pods, or at least groupings where students could talk to each other. Ultimately, the best I could manage was shifting the desks a little so people weren't staring directly at the back of someone else's head.

It is almost a certainty that your classroom will not have Internet access. At best, you may have secure Internet access, which is truly a good thing in prisons and still very rare. At worst, you will have either no computers or a classroom full of standalone machines. Your supervisor and the other instructors will be able to help navigate these situations. Technology access rules are different facility to facility so even if you are an experienced corrections educator, this will be an area of learning.

Depending on your program or class, access to supplies and materials may be an ongoing source of annoyance. What you bring in or out of the facility, other than your minimal personal property, is subject to scrutiny. Security has final say over what you can bring in for students, or not, and they may or may not give you an explanation for why they tell you no. This scrutiny extends to content, and you may find that articles, books, and magazines that you consider normal educational materials will be forbidden by security, with no recourse available. This is an area of ongoing frustration and conflict with prison staff; where we see prison culture and its suspicion of education on full display.

Vocational programs such as welding, carpentry, automotive repair, cosmetology, and barbering are common in prisons. They require extensive inventories of tools and supplies, many of which are small and mobile and considered security risks. These programs are monitored and secured, and the inventory is strictly controlled. Programs that are more hardware-dependent are often in secured areas, and may have security staff assigned mostly to them.

Programs and classes that require technology (printers, scanners, and computers) are monitored and secured also, but there is less concern that one of these larger items will be taken (although they could be disassembled for parts). The concerns around technology focus on access to information and systems, which is why incarcerated people have been denied access to the Internet and network technology. While there are pilot projects happening in a few states, the overall security response to people having online access has been a hard "no" for decades.

If you are teaching reading, writing, math, GED® classes, liberal arts courses, "soft" skills, yoga, or any type of class that does not require much beyond a few basic supplies will have few issues. Once your initial materials have been approved, you will leave them in the facility and only bring in more to replace what is used or worn out. Check with your supervisor or prison liaison if you want to add items, even things like colored paper.

If your facility allows students some freedom with school supplies, make sure you clear everything with your supervisor and security before you assign it to students. Highlighters and black pens, for example, are usually not allowed, so leave them out completely. If your students do not take anything from the classroom except their completed work, this shouldn't be a problem. If your students take books, binders, paper, and pens or pencils back and forth, you may want to be proactive in avoiding questions about property from security staff.

One way to try and prevent negative interactions over supplies is to include an inventory letter that lists everything students are allowed to have (and are responsible for returning) signed by all the appropriate people. Students should keep this letter close to hand, especially when there are new security staff around, or during rotation change while unfamiliar personnel settle into new positions. Any time something new is added, you should update the letter (and signatures) and give students a new copy. If you are teaching arts and crafts, you will need to have a regular procedure in place to check inventory and supplies, as well as communicate with staff about what students should have in their supply boxes.

One of the "problems" with issuing school supplies is that the commissary sells things like notebooks, pens, pencils, and so on. When a program gives these items to students, it becomes necessary to differentiate between a student's personal property (what they've purchased through the commissary) and program property (things students may not be allowed to keep, or would otherwise not have). You should be clear with students that they should not use the supplies they are given for schoolwork for their or their friends' personal use. As ludicrous as this may sound, it is a measure you can put in place to prevent students from using program supplies to engage in bartering, which is usually forbidden.

To illustrate this point: I and my clerks operated a stationary business for incarcerated women to buy non-commissary cards and prints as part of the program I was running. I employed artists (who were not students) and they were given a large box of art supplies to create art for stationary. Art is a common barter item and while I couldn't stop the artists from bartering their own art, I couldn't allow them to use program art supplies to create the art they bartered.

If security or prison administration thought that I was supplying artists with the means to create barter goods, the stationary program might have been shut down. I monitored the inventory and art product weekly, and created a way to mark program-related art so it couldn't be used as barter. It wasn't a perfect setup, but it was enough to show security I was making the effort to follow the rules. Issues still came up, but I generally was able to determine whether someone made a mistake or was attempting to manipulate the system.

Physically, your classroom or learning space is not yours. You don't have full control over how it is arranged, or what is available. If DOC has a contract with your program or agency, they also own the materials and supplies, unless they were purchased with other funding, and have the authority to say what you can and cannot do with all of them. In theory, this is not entirely different from the college owning everything in its classrooms. In practice, prisons are narrowly focused on control and risk avoidance, while colleges tend to be more open to exploration and risk-taking.

Establishing a Routine

Prisons are an interesting mix of strict routine and unpredictable variation. There are certain aspects of daily life that will remain fixed, and some that never seem to quite settle. Learning the routine of your facility and building will help you feel more settled, and will help the staff feel more comfortable with you. Establishing and maintaining a consistent, transparent routine will help build your credibility with security staff and students both.

Your daily routine will be more regimented than you may be used to, in part because prison routines will dictate when you have access to students, and when they can move around the facility. Although facilities can differ, it is likely your daily schedule (if you are teaching as part of agency-offered programming) will look something like this:

- Class for 2–2.5 hours in the morning
- Break for lunch, 1–1.5 hours
- Class for 2–2.5 hours in the afternoon

You may or may not have the same students morning and afternoon, depending on your class or program. The hours you are expected to be at work can vary, depending on what start and stop time will give you the most time in the classroom. Although you may prefer to work 9–5, for example, if students are available starting at 8:30, your schedule needs to adjust to theirs. Your daily routine should take into account two practical considerations: 1) you can never leave students without staff supervision and 2) you and they both need bathroom and water breaks.

Remember that students do not control their own time, nor can they move around in the facility of their own volition. They also cannot control other callouts, if their counselor or unit officer want to see them, or if their presence in required elsewhere by security. Unfortunately, you will likely **not** be notified about any of these and may have to ask other students, or spend time calling around to find out what happened. You will learn about how long it takes for everyone to get to class from their unit from the time they are allowed to leave, and it is appropriate to check in if people aren't showing up in that amount of time.

If you are a volunteer, you have to work when there is space and time available and may have little flexibility. You are also entirely subject to the prison schedule, which can shift abruptly, with no warning. If, for example, you have an evening class but there is an incident (say someone has a medical emergency and has to be taken out by ambulance), your class could get pushed back, shortened, or even cancelled. Unless you have someone in the facility who will give you a call, you probably won't be notified until you show up for class.

Evening classes can be a challenge as most of the day staff are gone and security may have a lighter duty roster. Your prison liaison may or may not be available in the evening, so make sure you know who to call or go to for both emergency and non-emergency situations. Once the day staff go home, evening personnel can have a harder time getting information. It would not be improbable for you to arrive, go to your room or space, and have only a few students (or none) show up but none of you knows why. Knowing who to call may not make you feel much better, but you will be able to make better decisions about what to do with your time.

It is normal to be nervous and perhaps feel a bit afraid your first few days. Carceral spaces are built to intimidate and disorient, and they are good at both. Although I haven't mentioned it before, prisons can also be unbelievably, unendingly noisy. Your classroom may be not be as noisy as other areas, but be prepared for constant intercom and security check interruptions. Learning the routines of the facility as well as the physical environment and layout will help you adjust to teaching inside.

Getting Started

I remember the first day I had students in the classroom. I had been working for a few weeks but hadn't started the class yet and I was nervous, uncertain what to expect or how to act. Some of my nervousness was new job jitters, combined with this strange environment, and the responsibility of running an entire program. But the majority came from not knowing how to act, what I could or couldn't say, and not knowing where I might royally fumble. My ears were full of dire warnings about manipulation, lying, discipline, and holding strong boundaries, to the point that I wasn't sure what I could actually say and not sound ridiculous.

I'm going to give you some guidelines, knowing that you will probably still feel all these things but hopefully to a lesser degree. The more confident and comfortable you appear the first time you meet your students, the sooner they will start feeling comfortable with you. My approach is to begin from a conservative starting point, as it is much harder to tighten things up after a casual beginning. I loosen up as I get more comfortable with the environment and establish a good rapport with my students.

If you are a person who likes to decorate their office space, or have personal mementos around, this is not the environment for extensive nesting behavior. Corrections culture generally discourages staff, especially front-line staff, from keeping pictures or other personal items visible to anyone who can look into your office. Agency staff often remove rings or other items related to family life, share minimal information about their lives outside of the prison, and actively discourage such questions.

If you like to decorate your classroom, check before hanging anything on the walls. Prisons often have strict guidelines around what content is allowed, as well as what materials can be used on the walls themselves. You may also want to wait and ask your students what kind of classroom environment they would most appreciate.

Before You Meet Your Students

It took months before I had a basic understanding of how I could and could not interact with my students. If you go through a corrections training as part of a new employee onboarding, you will hear some of this, but the framing will be very different. If you are an experienced corrections educator, you may already know these and whether you have to adhere to them strictly or if there is a bit of flexibility in your facility. My advice is always to start off from a more conservative and formal position, then adjust as you learn.

There are three types of social interaction that cause problems for people new to carceral environments: general communication, names, and sharing personal information. Each of these has invisible pitfalls specific to the corrections environment, but that are an accepted part of everyday life outside and in free classrooms. All three of these situations are, under different circumstances, part of building a relationship and include different types of friendly intimacy, both physical and verbal.

Relationship-Building

Safe relationships with students cannot progress to **any** level of intimacy. You can be kind, welcoming, and compassionate, but you cannot be intimate, in either a friendly or romantic way. This can be a challenging aspect of corrections teaching to navigate, as much of our relationship-building behavior is nonverbal and unconscious. It is normal to desire connections with others but in carceral spaces those connections are closely monitored and constrained.

These are guidelines you can use to help with this boundary, at least until you are more familiar with your facility's environment and expectations:

- No physical contact beyond handshakes or occasional high fives.
- No private conversation or communication. Follow the Rule of Three (i.e., three people in the room) or make sure you are in line of sight of a window or open door at all times. Even if you are meeting for office hours, make sure there is another person present, or that other staff can easily hear or see you talking. Do not compromise on this because it is inconvenient.
- Do NOT send personal notes or communication to your students via kyte, kiosk, JPay, letters, or any other mode of communication, including via family members or friends (yours or theirs).

- Do not keep or share secrets. Students should know that anything they tell you is not confidential from other staff or employees, and that you must report anything illegal, unethical, or abusive. On the reverse, you should never share personal secrets with your students. *I cannot emphasize this enough—you are putting their safety at risk as well as your own.* **Don't do it**.

Names

Consider how you want to be addressed and how you want to address your students. Almost anything that includes your last name is fine—Professor, Doctor, Mr/Ms, but asking students to use your first name is likely to draw unwanted attention. Most corrections staff address people by last name; sometimes honorific and last name. I recommend going with honorific and last name for yourself, but you will have to decide on how to address your students.

I did not encourage nicknames or pet names in student to student interactions, although I did not monitor private conversations. I recommend this in part to encourage more structured behavior, and for students to separate their classroom life from their life on the tier or unit.

I asked my class and my program clerks about this and we disagreed at first. I took a more formal approach, but eventually went to first names in the classroom. If I needed to refer to students outside the classroom, I used last names only to comply with security conventions. It is much easier to start more formally and relax the convention than the reverse. Names are important in prisons, do not underestimate the impact of addressing people in a respectful, caring manner and expecting the same from them.

Personal Information

The earlier advice about limiting personal items in your office extends to sharing personal information with students. I find that a good approach in any situation with skewed power dynamics is to name the issue and set the boundary early. When it comes to personal information, the best advice is to share none, or as little as possible. However, sharing personal information is one of the ways we build relationships with people, so sharing none is impractical.

Instead, I consider that information about my experience in education—as a student, working in a college, or teaching—is shareable. I use those experiences to give students examples of scenarios, test taking, resolving conflict with teachers, and working with other students. I knew that anything I said in the classroom might be repeated and overheard by corrections staff, so I shared with that in mind. I also knew that corrections staff could walk into the classroom at any moment and listen to anything we were discussing.

This is a hard boundary to set and maintain and everyone has to make their own decisions about what to share or not share. Keep in mind that if corrections staff start to believe that you are sharing too much or developing inappropriate relationships, you may come under scrutiny. This can jeopardize your students and your position, and potentially have consequences for your program or department. Sharing information and building trust in an environment that views all such things with automatic suspicion is not easy, but it is doable.

One good guideline is whether you would want your supervisor or any corrections staff to be in the room when you are sharing information. If your answer isn't a strong "sure," then don't share. I have a two-part boundary for sharing information generally:

Part one: It is best to avoid specific or personal details about anything—you, your history, hobbies, family, and so on. I would often generalize an experience I had, or relationships, but never shared specifics about my life or interests. I did share educational experiences (i.e., I'm not good at multiple choices tests, they're really hard) but no details about schools I attended or where I lived when I was in school. Sharing these kinds of details can be misinterpreted as a type of intimacy, or friendliness, that is not allowable in a prison setting.

Part two is being clear that I will not answer questions about myself or my life beyond what I have shared. I am clear with students about this at the start of class, and give them one or two slip-ups before enforcing the boundary.

It is inevitable that someone will forget, or will test my willingness to enforce what I've said, but making this statement up front means enforcing the boundary is easier. If a student is insistent, I ask them if, given that I set the boundary and have given a warning, if they think they are making a good decision by continuing to insist. I do not make this a private conversation—if they try to violate my boundary in public, I will remind them in public—I never laugh it off, shame them, or pretend they didn't ask.

Your facility may have rules that address sharing personal information. If it does, make sure you follow them. You could put something in the syllabus, similar to the academic code of conduct, and go over it with them. It will likely feel uncomfortable, but it is for your protection and theirs. Acknowledging the discomfort of limiting the relationship in this way is a good starting point for a conversation about classroom dynamics.

Classroom Dynamics

All classrooms have their challenges and, to some degree, each of the dynamics noted here is present in all of organized education's spaces. I mention them because, like everything in prison, your actions can have unintended consequences beyond poor grades or someone failing a class. You cannot avoid taking action, nor can you eliminate these challenges entirely, although you can reduce their influence. Your primary goal is to create a space where these dynamics are less present, and the expansive energy of learning is predominant.

Undercurrents

One major difference between free campus classrooms and prison classrooms is that people in free campus classes don't all live together. In prison, they do. They may not live in the same cell or bunk area but, at the least, they live in the same complex, possibly in the same unit or tier. This constant, unrelenting proximity can lead to a spiderweb of relationships and conflicts, most existing outside of your classroom, many extending outside the prison. This intricate web of relationships can lead to strong undercurrents in the classroom, especially until students understand your boundaries and expectations.

Programming classrooms are one of the few places people who do not live in the same living area get to see each other and interact. In the early stages of building a classroom community, you may have to give more attention to interpersonal dynamics than you will later. Groups naturally go through periods of conflict, just as they go through phases of calm creativity, and you need to be prepared for both. Prisons, especially male facilities, have strict hierarchies and even in the classroom, these may occasionally surface.

Setting a clearly defined expectation that people treat each other with dignity and courtesy is the starting point in managing potential conflicts. It is inevitable that aspects of prison culture such as racial divisions, hyper-masculinity, or personal conflicts are present in the space. You don't need to know details and, in most cases, are better off not asking. Approaching conflicts with a neutral demeanor, and expecting that students will demonstrate good-faith behavior is a strong tool.

I am not encouraging deliberate blindness or naivete, but some aspects of prison life are beyond your ability to influence or resolve. Learning that a disagreement stems from long-standing conflict between different factions, or that people are unhappy about changes in schedules or commissary items doesn't settle the disruption to the learning space. If needed, you can gather more information after the classroom is resettled.

Power and Control

Prisons are an extreme example of "power over" institutions, where the illusion of safety is maintained by physical constraint and the constant threats of violence and force as a way to maintain order. In prison or jail, trust is a scare commodity, and educators can never assume that people will trust them simply because they are a teacher. In fact, many people may trust even less, depending on the amount of educational trauma they have suffered. When we layer this with racist, ableist systems, students in prison classrooms may have little ability or desire to trust teachers and other authority figures, especially those of races and ethnicities different from theirs.

In prisons, domination is the model for interaction and relationship, and incarcerated people learn that lesson quickly. If you have not examined and actively worked to dismantle your own indoctrination into the Dominator model of teaching, you will not only replicate it, it will ultimately be a tool of your assimilation into prison culture. You do not have to brutalize people to dehumanize them, just as you do not have to brutalize yourself. You can simply stop paying attention, stop engaging in self-reflection and calling yourself to account for your classroom choices. You can choose to accept that since you hold absolute authority in the space, whatever you do must be fine, no matter its impact on the people in the room.

Incarcerated people live in a world where they cannot say "no" without some form of consequence. Staff are in positions of absolute authority and there are rules and procedures in place to govern almost every type of interaction. Where there are no rules, corrections culture has filled the gap with invisible norms and mores that dictate what is acceptable and what isn't. One of your biggest challenges will be to traverse this combination of rules and culture, while remembering your humanity, your students', and that of other staff.

Your students are experts at navigating and surviving a situation where they have very little power or control. In an environment where staff are almost always given the benefit of the doubt, students are unlikely to exercise their right to speak freely, disagree, or challenge something they see as wrong or unfair. This can inhibit your ability to increase their critical thinking skills unless you are adept and thoughtful in creating a settled environment.

Institutionalization

Institutionalization, which is not unique to carceral spaces, "…is an often-deliberate process where a person entering the institution is reprogrammed to accept and conform to strict controls that enable the institution to manage a large number of people with a minimum of necessary staff" (Haney, 2001). The process of institutionalization became even more pronounced when the United States began its mass incarceration policies in the late 1980s and early 1990s. Ratios of incarcerated persons to staff can be as high as 80 to 1, and the impact of this type of stress on corrections staff cannot be underestimated (Changing Minds, n.d.).

Institutionalization was not created by prisons or corrections, but is a tool well-suited to Euro-white systems and the Dominator dynamic, and key element of corrections culture.

Organized education itself requires a measure of institutionalization, as teachers are trained to dominate and control classrooms, and administrators dominate and control their staff. Many of us who have experience organized education have gotten a taste of being forced to adopt behaviors and thinking patterns that do not align with how we experience and understand the world. The school-to-prison pipeline is one of the manifestations of BIPOC and disabled children's attempts to resist educational institutionalization.

People who have gone through treatment programs, the foster care system, spent time in mental health facilities, monasteries, and the military have also experienced institutionalization. To this date, at best, we have a piecemeal approach to de-institutionalization, with almost no research and only an anecdotal understanding of how to help people recover from forced assimilation. Forced assimilation into the institution results in habits and behaviors which are detrimental when people eventually return to the community.

These habits and behaviors are designed to weaken autonomy and increase fear, thereby reducing access to executive functions. For people who leave prison wanting to fashion new lives for themselves and make different choices, the changes that happen in the brain during institutionalization have serious negative implications. The constant presence of stress hormones and chemicals, combined with punishment for critical thinking, questioning, and acting independently can only weaken the connections between the amygdala and prefrontal cortex, impacting, for example, people's decision making and critical thinking.

There are numerous elements of institutionalization and they produce a variety of identifiable impacts on behavior. Changing Minds, referenced earlier, provides a useful description of the steps of institutionalization. These are four I consider most relevant to people's ability to learn as they result in behaviors and attitudes that consistently undermine learning, especially in college classrooms:

- Depersonalize: weakens identity; process of dehumanization begins with assigning numbers to replace names and refusing to acknowledge individual identity.
- Destroy the self: disconnection from prior life; individual goods are replaced with those identical to everyone else's, rendering people invisible in the group.
- Control all aspects of life: remove meaningful choices; decisions are superficial, with no real impact on quality of life or future.
- Force obedience: maintain constant, low-level threat; ongoing state of hypervigilance results in extended stress response which limits access to executive functions.

The following is a list of different ways institutionalization can show up in classrooms and impact learning. There is not a direct, one-to-one correlation to the steps of institutionalization, although the connections are clear.

- Weak decision-making: People appear to want to be told what to do. If they are given the opportunity to make decisions, they may decide entirely on impulse, or be unable to describe their decision-making process. When asked about why they made a particular decision, they may become defensive and agitated.
- Elevated threat response: People are hypersensitive to cues and may be severely dysregulated, unable to calm and settle their nervous system. This shows up in many ways, often as physical agitation, and a need to control the immediate physical environment.
- Extremes of behavior around authority: People present as disassociated and passive or forward and aggressive, often with very little moderation. The more authority is exercised, the more extreme the behavior.

- Lack of emotional responsivity: People become de-sensitized to the suffering or deeper emotional states of themselves and others. Showing certain emotions is considered a sign of weakness in men's prisons, and most people (both incarcerated people and staff) develop a flat affect as a survival tactic.

There is even less information about the impacts of incarceration and institutionalization on learning, either during or after release. The research that exists on education and incarceration focuses mainly on connections between education, employment and recidivism (albeit with major gaps in understanding as to what is effective and why), with rising scholarship on the importance of access to education beyond vocational and trades training for incarcerated people.

Moments of Choice

In these environments—prisons, jails, detention centers, and other types of lockdown facilities—there are things you should know. Depending on how much time you spend in the facility, you will, to some degree normalize things you would never think you could and internalize the narrative of control and domination. You will also come to a point when you realize that staying means finding ways to compartmentalize (and disengage from) the individual and systemic harm to yourself and others.

I know educators who have worked in facilities, full time, for decades. They believe in their work, are dedicated, and treat students with respect. You may have the capability and talent for a long-term career in corrections education that doesn't dehumanize your students or you, or you may not. I did not, and still do not, have the capacity to work long-term in a carceral space. I can't say with any confidence why that is but I know for me, I faced a moment of choice.

I knew that in order to continue working in that system I would have to make some fundamental change, a change that would alter how I thought about and interacted with my students. I would have to allow a measure of distance to open up between myself and them; to become less proximate to their joy in learning, and to their suffering. I was unable, and uninterested, in making that change. I believe that the first moment of choice comes and that choice can set a pattern for all the future moments.

Choosing unconsciously is rarely a wise way to make decisions. Unconscious choices can take us down pathways of increasing disconnection and dehumanization, embedding us in a culture of great harm. Pay attention to yourself and to your inner cautions and questions. Your moment may sneak up on you, quietly, or it may burst through the door with its hair on fire—just don't overlook or ignore its presence.

Where does the pathway of unconscious choice lead? At its best, if a person's core of decency and compassion is large enough that they continuing treating students well, it can lead to a career of decent work and solid teaching. At its worst, teachers replicate the brutality and dehumanization they see and experience daily, without realizing what has happened to them. Realizing you have been perpetuating cycles of harm and trauma can be a crushing moment, and difficult to recover from.

The story I'm sharing happened while I was working as a reentry education navigator. For people who have worked inside, it may seem familiar. It is a good illustration of why I was unable to continue working inside, as the number of considerations I ran through before deciding on a course of action twisted my brain and heart into knots.

Today, I got a letter from a young man in a facility I'd visited recently. Getting correspondence is not unusual, although I don't get a lot of letters, but this was like nothing I'd ever gotten before. This letter had nothing to do with my job or education, but about rumors he'd heard that he was going to be murdered.

How do you describe a moment that surreal? When a letter opens with *"this doesn't have anything to do with the questions I asked while you were here"* and ends with *"I don't have anywhere else to turn, will you please call DOC headquarters and tell them all these things?"* It should be a no-brainer. Call DOC and report the letter, it's all over, that's what almost anyone would do, with no hesitation.

But that's not what I did, at least not at first. The first thing I did was talk through the implications of this extraordinary piece of communication with a colleague and try to piece out potential consequences of whatever decision I made. I know that may sound overly cautious, so let's break down what those outcomes might be, given the claim and the communication. I want you to better understand my hesitation and decision-making process, because there is a chance you will find yourself in a situation like this at least once.

> If letter was a prank, then DOC would inflict punishment. I was likely not going to get into trouble, but DOC might decide to limit my access to students inside, or limit them contacting me.
>
> If the letter was an attempt to manipulate me into advocating for them in some way, DOC would administer punishment and I might be drawn in further in their attempt to investigate. If manipulation were the goal, the chance of losing access to students increased.
>
> If the letter was genuine, then there was a person so afraid for their safety that they wanted me (a complete stranger they interacted with for one or two minutes, several months back) to call DOC, as an intermediary, and request steps be taken.
>
> A normal process should be that a person this fearful would make such a request themselves, but I had no way of knowing what had already happened. Perhaps the person had already made a request but was denied, don't want to be seen talking with DOC personnel about anything, or are afraid of DOC staff. With no information and no way to get any, I had to decide based on only the letter.

I also took into consideration the bleaker knowledge that DOC could decide to either ignore the request, or lock the person into segregation for an unspecified amount of time "for their own safety." The person had to know this was a likely outcome, perhaps it was what they wanted. Ultimately, I called the prison and made a formal report, despite my many misgivings, because there was a reasonable chance it was a genuine request for help. I never found out what happened and that story hasn't gotten easier to remember with time.

Conscious, thoughtful work in carceral spaces can require this kind of mind-bending decision making. Corrections staff often assume incarcerated people are lying or manipulating to get what they want, and reactions come from that assumption rather than a true consideration of the person's needs. Incarcerated people do sometimes lie or manipulate as a way to get their needs met in a system that considers them less than human. Determining the best course of action in a culture determined to control, dehumanize, and assume the worst often means taking the least bad option—the one that leads to the least amount of punishment or staff reactivity for the incarcerated person.

Unconscious decision making hides us from the consequences of those decisions. If we don't acknowledge there was a decision and that we made it, whatever happened just….happened. We can pretend that it is the fault of the system, and the system is too big for one person to change. Not trying seems easier, in part because we internalize the mythology that DOC is all-powerful, that we are at risk of being targeted by the system if we attempt to intervene.

But that does not make us less culpable, or less responsible for

- not advocating for someone who is being targeted by guards, even when you know they're being targeted;
- letting people give up because they're just too difficult or abrasive in the classroom;
- punishing instead of asking questions and helping a student seek assistance;
- not constantly searching for ways to expose students to new and interesting material;
- laughing at "prisoner" jokes, or telling them yourself;
- looking the other way when staff bully or intimidate incarcerated people or other staff;
- letting your discomfort with people's anxiety and stress leak out as impatience or condescension, treating them as "prisoners" instead of students;
- Googling students' names after work so you can tourist in on their past mistakes and suffering.

The list of dehumanizing choices is endless. These are a few I've witnessed, some from well-meaning people, and all represent a moment of decision. Do we treat people with dignity and acknowledge their humanity, or do we look aside?

The moral authority we assume because we are not, ourselves, incarcerated, is not authority but superiority. Moral superiority, which is often paired with white saviorism (especially in white women), is one of the by-products of the Dominator matrix, and quickly becomes a pathway to assimilation into corrections culture.

Once you accept the myth that you are the only and final authority in the classroom, it takes only a breath to stop believing that your students are human. Why would you think of them as human when you no longer truly consider yourself as human? Following the example of organized education, you become the expert in your small domain, unassailable and infallible, no longer an imperfect, fallible human. Challenge, which is what we should expect from people who are stretching and growing their minds, hearts, and spirits, is no longer acceptable and must be punished.

I was a student for two and a half decades before I finished my master's degree. I encountered this attitude in free college classrooms over and over, although to a lesser degree, and with far less harmful impacts. In free classrooms, students can challenge this attitude, although a fair outcome is by no means assured. A student voice may also remind the teacher of their shared humanity, and that we can create equitable, courteous ways to resolve our differences. In the end, free students have the right to simply leave—to disengage—and continue to live their lives.

In the prison classroom, you are responsible for maintaining your own humanity, and remembering the humanity of others. Maintain rigorous standards as you create room for students to practice accountability, make mistakes, and rediscover their learning selves. Create and actively pursue a practice of self-reflection and development that can sustain you while working in such a bleak environment. Above all, give your students as much freedom and choice as possible, and treat them with dignity no matter the circumstances.

References

Alexander, M. (2012). *The new Jim Crow*. New York, NY: The New Press.

American Civil Liberties Union. (n.d.). *School-to-prison pipeline*. Retrieved from https://www.aclu.org/issues/juvenile-justice/school-prison-pipeline

Armstrong, G., Atkin Plunk, C. A., & Wells, J. (2015). The relationship between work–family conflict, correctional officer job stress, and job satisfaction. *Criminal Justice and Behavior, 42*(10), 1066–1082. DOI: 10.1177/0093854815582221

Cantora, A. (2020). *Congress lifts long-standing ban on Pell grants to people in prison*. Retrieved from PBS.org: https://www.pbs.org/newshour/education/congress-lifts-long-standing-ban-on-pell-grants-to-people-in-prison

Changing Minds. (n.d.). *Institutionalization*. Retrieved from http://changingminds.org/disciplines/sociology/articles/institutionalization.htm

Couloute, L. (2018). *Getting back on course: Educational exclusion and attainment among formerly incarcerated people*. Prison Policy Initiative. Retrieved from https://www.prisonpolicy.org/reports/education.html

Davis, A. Y. (2003). *Are prisons obsolete?*. New York, NY: Seven Stories Press.

Department of Justice Office of Justice Programs. (n.d.). *Prison rape elimination act, overview*. Retrieved from https://bja.ojp.gov/program/prison-rape-elimination-act-prea/overview

Enns, P., Yi, Y., Comfort, M., Goldman, A., Lee, H., Muller, C., & Wildeman, C. (2019). What percentage of Americans have ever had a family member incarcerated?: Evidence from the family history of incarceration survey. *Socius*. DOI:10.1177/2378023119829332

Gray, L.-A. (2016). *The spectrum of educational trauma*. Retrieved from https://www.huffpost.com/entry/the-spectrum-of-education_b_8619536

Gray, L.-A. (2019). *Educational trauma*. Cham, Switzerland: Palgrave Macmillan.

Haney, C. (2001). *The psychological impact of incarceration: Implications for post-prison adjustment. Office of the assistant secretary for planning and evaluation*. US Department of Health and Human Services. Retrieved from https://aspe.hhs.gov/reports/psychological-impact-incarceration-implications-post-prison-adjustment-0

Harlow, P. C. (2003). *Bureau of justice statistics: Education and correctional populations*. Department of Justice, Office of Justice Programs. Retrieved from https://www.bjs.gov/content/pub/pdf/ecp.pdf

International Corrections and Prisons Association. (n.d.). *U.S. Department of education launches second chance pell pilot program for incarcerated individuals*. Retrieved from https://icpa.org/u-s-department-of-education-launches-second-chance-pell-pilot-program-for-incarcerated-individuals/

Kaba, M. (2021). *We do this 'til we free us: Abolitionist organizing and transforming justice (Abolitionist Papers)*. Chicago, IL: Haymarket Books.

Kara, J. (2017). *Inmate GEDs drop off after test goes online*. Retrieved from https://ctmirror.org/2017/12/28/inmate-geds-drop-off-after-test-goes-online/

Levine, S. (2018). *2020 Census will continue to count prisoners where they are incarcerated*. Retrieved from www.huffingtonpost.com: https://www.huffingtonpost.com/entry/2020-census-prison-population_us_5a7cb966e4b044b3821b0507

Love, B. (2019). *We want to do more than survive: Abolitionist teaching and the pursuit of educational freedom*. Boston, MA: Beacon Press.

Menakem, R. (2017). *My grandmother's hands*. Las Vegas, NV: Central Recovery Press.

Mendez, E. (2017). *Passing rate on GED plummets*. Retrieved from https://urbanmilwaukee.com/2017/05/23/passing-rate-on-ged-has-plummeted/

Milloy, C. (2016). *How American oligarchs created the concept of race to divide and conquer the poor*. Retrieved from https://www.washingtonpost.com/local/how-wealthy-americans-divided-and-conquered-the-poor-to-create-the-concept-of-race/2016/04/19/2cab6e38-0643-11e6-b283-e79d81c63c1b_story.html

National PREA Resource Center. (n.d.). Prison Rape Elimination Act. Retrieved from https://www.prearesourcecenter.org/about/prison-rape-elimination-act

Office of the Inspector General. (2005). *Deterring staff sexual abuse of federal inmates*. Retrieved from https://oig.justice.gov/sites/default/files/archive/special/0504/index.htm

Penal labor in the United States. (n.d.). Retrieved from https://en.wikipedia.org/wiki/Penal_labor_in_the_United_States

Prison Gerrymandering Project. (2018). *The problem*. Retrieved from https://www.prisonersofthecensus.org/impact.html

Ruiz, E. (2020). Structural trauma. *Meridians: Feminism, race, transnationalism* (Forthcoming), *20*(2), 1–15. Retrieved from https://philarchive.org/archive/RUZST

Straker D. (2010). *Institutionalization*. Retrieved from http://changingminds.org/disciplines/sociology/articles/institutionalization.htm

Strauss, V. (2015). *The big problems with Pearson's new GED high school equivalency test*. Retrieved from https://www.washingtonpost.com/news/answer-sheet/wp/2015/07/09/the-big-problems-with-pearsons-new-ged-high-school-equivalency-test/?noredirect=on

Substance Abuse and Mental Health Services Administration. (2014). *Treatment improvement protocol* (TIP) Series, No. 57. Appendix C, historical account of trauma. Trauma-informed care in behavioral health services. Retrieved from https://www.ncbi.nlm.nih.gov/books/NBK207202/

The Moral Injury Project. (n.d.). *What is moral injury?* Retrieved from https://moralinjuryproject.syr.edu/about-moral-injury/

Thompson, H. A. (2013). *How prisons change the balance of power in America*. Retrieved from https://www.theatlantic.com/national/archive/2013/10/how-prisons-change-the-balance-of-power-in-america/280341/

United States Department of Justice. (2012). *Prison rape elimination Act PRISONS AND JAIL STANDARDS United States Department of Justice Final Rule*. Retrieved from https://bja.ojp.gov/sites/g/files/xyckuh186/files/media/document/PREA-Prison-Jail-Standards.pdf

Vera Institute of Justice. (2020). *Department of education announces expansion of second chance pell experimental sites initiative, selecting 67 new postsecondary education in prison sites*. Retrieved from https://www.vera.org/newsroom/department-of-education-announces-expansion-of-second-chance-pell-experimental-sites-initiative-selecting-67-new-postsecondary-education-in-prison-sites

Vyse, M. (2012). *Why a privatized GED will fail students*. Retrieved from https://socialistworker.org/2012/12/11/a-privatized-ged-fails-students

Wartenweiler, T. (2017). Trauma-informed education: An interpretative phenomenological analysis. *The Online Journal of New Horizons in Education, 7*(2), 96–106.

Chapter 5

Learning to Expand

Survival is the work of the body, but learning is the work of the soul. The desire to survive and the desire to learn and grow are always striving—sometimes balanced and sometimes not. Trauma impacts and constrains our ability to learn, but because the human brain and spirit have such a strong desire for growth and expansion, many people learn, grow, and create despite the trauma they carry. When the desire and work of survival hinder dampen the ability to learn, the DESIRE to learn does not cease. We want to encourage that desire to flourish and thrive.

In Chapter 3, the Points of Entry diagram illustrates that our work on trauma - how we think about, envision, and reimagine the nature of harm, resilience, healing, integration, and resolution—can vastly exceed what we have imagined. Settling and expanding through learning is a new vision for addressing a different set of traumatic impacts, approaching its acceptance and integration from new perspectives. In this light, education and learning are natural and instinctive forms of traumatic intervention; recovery processes that consider learning how to learn, and "reshaping the learner identity" (Wartenweiler 2017), as a necessary and worthwhile purpose in and of themselves.

To bring this imagining into reality, we must reshape teaching and learning.

Reshaping how we think about teaching and learning means that we treat ourselves as full human beings, not just content delivery systems. Who we are and how we move through the world are as important as our content expertise. If we are full of unaddressed rage and pain and shame, we will transmit that dirty pain to our students, continuing cycles of trauma and oppression. Tending to our own wounds and unaddressed pain, resolving to work on our personal struggles helps us as people, and also begins to end cycles of educational trauma.

Lightbulb Moments

If you've been teaching for a while, you'll understand when I say that there are times when you and your students hit a groove. The physical energy in the room feels warm and comfortable, you may get a tingling sensation at the top of your head, or around your head and shoulders, and you can almost feel every mind in the room concentrated on whatever it is you are all sharing. This can happen in groups or one on one and it almost always happens before someone has that "lightbulb" moment we all love so much. I hope that you've experienced this at least once, perhaps as both a teacher and a student. It's a moment of pure magic and connection and meaning-making, and is probably the reason many of you are reading this book.

I experience those lightbulb moments as leaps forward in ability to learn, not just mastery of a concept or task. People master concepts and complete tasks all the time, but lightbulb moments are precious and rare, and we treasure them. When I imagine lightbulb moments, I envision trust, connection, acceptance, curiosity, and the desire to explore, all coming together simultaneously around whatever we are striving to grasp.

DOI: 10.4324/9781003048312-5

When those elements align, it is like we push through an invisible barrier and POP, we're in a new place! We leveled up! What if these moments are what it feels like when we create a set of new neural pathways and connections, expanding our capacity for learning and integration? Experience shows that leveling up through layers and layers of traumatic experience is harder, but those who do it bring a powerful and entirely new integrated perspective into the world.

These moments cannot happen in the presence of fear and, as hooks reminds us (always), fear leaves in the presence of love (2001). In the same text, hooks, referencing Peck, describes love as "the will to extend one's self for the purpose of nurturing one's own or another's spiritual growth" (p. 4). In carceral settings, love requires a redefinition—a method of expression that can exist and thrive in a hostile environment. For educators, building a learner's confidence in themselves, in their ability to relate well to others, and in their own value is a profound demonstration of love, amplifying the definition shared by hooks and Peck.

Mariame Kaba speaks to the necessity of hope and the choice to trust. Hope, she says, is a practice and daily discipline, as is the choice to trust people until they prove themselves untrustworthy (2021). Where these elements intersect—love, belief in growth and change, hope, trust, and commitment to vigorous practice—is where expansive learning exists and leads to a future arising from our best creative moments.

Finding our way to these moments in carceral classrooms, holding space for our students to find their way to these moments, is the resolute and joyful magic we all need. It is expansive learning manifested, a physical and energetic marker of our hearts, minds, and souls working together to create an explosion of growth and light.

Trauma-Responsive Education

Trauma-responsive education first attempts to mitigate harm through interrupting the historic and systemic trauma intrinsic to organized education. Specifically, trauma-responsive education requires that teachers and educators acknowledge that educational trauma is embedded in every aspect of organized education in the United States, both K–12 and adult education. Trauma-responsive educators make it their work to understand and acknowledge this harm, building learning spaces and personal practice that directly counter its effects on learning, especially for incarcerated and system-impacted students.

Next, we respond with an approach that

1   Adapts current best practices from the field of Trauma-Informed Care to the needs of learning spaces.
2   Emphasizes settling and expanding as foundations for strengthening ability to learn.
3   Requires teachers' commitment to rigorous self-care and reflection as a necessary component for interrupting educational trauma cycles.
4   Recenters joy and imagination in adult classrooms.

With this approach, we can co-create spaces where the process of learning is as meaningful, or more so, than content. In prison, content can lose its immediacy, especially when students have no way to apply that learning in their daily lives. Trauma-responsive practice offers learning beyond content; internal, self-directed exploration that students can engage as part of the work of their lives.

Integration of anything—new materials, philosophies, ways of knowing—is rarely easy but my experience so far is that teachers see this as work worth doing. The responses from seasoned educators have been positive and encouraging. Corrections educators in particular are desperate to understand why adult students so eager to learn run into seemingly inexplicable barriers. Making this shift, transforming ourselves and our spaces, is risky, and we do not know what to expect from this unknown venture.

My experience was that students began to feel more confident and believe in themselves as learners, and this often led to upswings in grades, but not in all cases. I observed their interactions with each other, and with me, were less fraught with anxiety and for some, this increased confidence transferred into other areas of their lives. Other students were less consistent, or seemed comfortable with change only in the classroom environment; some were uninterested in anything not strictly intellectual and did their best to avoid interacting even with other students. I did my best to meet each of them where they were, although I am certain I pushed harder than I might now.

They discovered that the intellectual aspect of learning was easier than they expected. Once they had a few successes, even small ones, behind them, their curiosity and craving for learning exploded. I was constantly seeking or creating new activities and projects to satisfy their desire for learning, and was barely able to stay a few steps ahead. Even projects I considered challenging did not challenge them for long as I worked with extremely gifted and intelligent people.

Like all classrooms, I had a small handful of students who continually struggled. I have not looked into the science, but I believe there are certain aspects of learning that are harder to repair after intense trauma and/or substance use. I know the students I had who struggled the most academically had similar backgrounds and demonstrated similar problems with learning. They were capable, but needed more time and a different approach, neither of which I could provide. They could have redeveloped their learning skills with time, patience, and intensive work, although what that would mean academically is unknown.

Considering Gender

I mentioned gender in the Introduction because gendered research on incarceration is extremely limited. My teaching work inside was with women, although I worked mostly with men during my tenure as an education and reentry navigator, and I have taught mixed-gender classes throughout my teaching career. Men's and women's prisons are different in many ways, including cultural expectations, norms, and behaviors.

On a free campus, teachers in mixed-gender classrooms might not consider gender when they are developing lesson plans and activities but corrections educators need to consider it more closely. Prison culture (which is different than corrections culture but also influences all aspects of social and daily life for incarcerated people) defines and enforces rigid codes of behavior, and those codes cannot be easily disregarded. Consequences, at the worst, can be violent and life-threatening. Even lesser consequences can result in loss of face and relationships, isolation, bullying, and harassment. If you ask (or require) students to act in ways contrary to prison codes and norms, they may not feel they can refuse, even if it jeopardizes their safety.

It may be, for example, that you want ask male students to use "feeling words" during daily check-ins. In many spaces, this is a routine activity and is done as a way to increase emotional vocabulary, bring people into their bodies and connect with their emotional state. Your intention is good, but until students have come to trust you and each other, publicly sharing "feeling words" may not be a popular activity. Having them do warm-up writing or drawing exercises instead could achieve the same end, but would not require public vulnerability.

I used male students for that example, but the same could be true for female students. A good general approach is to protect student dignity and privacy as much as possible, and let them indicate when they are ready to share more openly. Increasing your understanding of gender and learning as well as the norms and codes your students live with may increase their comfort level with your classroom expectations.

Movement in the Classroom

The importance of movement in trauma work (from any point of entry) cannot be underestimated (Menakem, 2017; Porges, 2014; van der Kolk, 2014) but, at best, options for using movement are very limited in carceral spaces (other than approved programming or recreation). Despite its importance, movement is not mentioned in the framework for this reason. Because control of the physical body is central to corrections, movement of that body is subject to intense scrutiny. Not all movement is forbidden, but you must be extremely thoughtful in deciding what to offer students. Any movement practice you encourage must be small, contained, and focused on settling in the classroom.

At the very beginning of my time working inside, I had thought I would teach my students some dance steps as a way to build community and move our bodies. When I mentioned this plan to a co-worker, they told me immediately that this kind of movement was strictly forbidden by corrections culture and the code of conduct. Recreational movement (i.e., some team sports, fitness activities, and (usually) volunteer-led activities like yoga) in both men and women's facilities are allowed, but only within specified parameters and locations. My classroom was not one of those locations.

Considering the physical impact of trauma on the body, the long-term, intergenerational impacts of disallowing people to bodily release trauma is overwhelming. Porges tells us that when we are in a defensive posture (feeling threatened and/or unsafe), mammals must move. If we are confined (i.e., isolated or restrained), our nervous system defaults to immobilization, possibly dissociation. Consequences from the system are not the only reason to take great care with any movement practice.

Prisons are NOT a safe places to process trauma that may be released by intensive body work or specific types of movement.

If you do want to incorporate physical activity, do so as a settling exercise, not as trauma–release work. There are a number of ways to help students bring themselves into the state of inner calm, or restful vitality, that is conducive to learning such as tapping, chair yoga, breathing exercises, doodling, or drawing.

Box 5.1   Note on movement

Go through any movement activity before class and make sure you are comfortable with everything on the list—saying the words and performing the physical movements.

If you aren't comfortable, they won't be either.

I find that students are more willing to try something new if they can control when and how they experiment. Making instructions or guidelines available to everyone via posters or handouts (if allowed) ensures everyone has access to what they need, when they need it, without having to let anyone else know.

Provide written instructions and phrases students can repeat to themselves, then go through the movements once or twice as a class. This gives students cover to learn quietly and in a way that may preserve dignity. Talk with them about what movement in the classroom is acceptable and set expectations early. I spoke with my students often about the importance of letting the body move during learning, even if that movement is not entirely free. We talked about different learning styles (even though I know there is disagreement amongst researchers on this subject) and I found that many students were strong kinesthetic learners. Movement, including writing, doodling, note-taking, and typing helped them on multiple levels.

Allowing your students to use their bodies to settle themselves internally, as opposed to only meditative or intellect-based practices, builds trust and increases their sense of personal autonomy, even if the movement is small. Talking with them about why you think this kind of practice is important, explaining what it means and how it can help them (instead of just directing them to do it) may get you more participation. Encouraging students to integrate their settling practice elsewhere in their lives will help them when they are studying and learning outside the classroom also.

The Framework

The topic of trauma has exploded into the mainstream in the last few years and shows every sign of becoming a permanent part of every type of helping profession. The demand for information on both the science and application has permeated almost every field of study and practice that relates to caring for and working with people. However we integrate trauma work into our teaching, in carceral spaces we must remember that,

- Students may have extensive, unaddressed trauma histories that cannot be safely accessed in a non-mental health, group setting.
- Prisons are not safe, your students do not physically control their bodies or environment. Your classroom may offer a respite, but your students still live in a carceral environment.
- We are free; we get to go home.

This general lack of safety, or feeling safe, presents us with a puzzle: *How do we advance learning if students, given their backgrounds and the environment, are in a constant, low-level state of fear and internal unease?*

Pursuing the answer to that question led me to the principles of Trauma-informed Care (TIC) as put forth by Hummer, Dollard, Robst, Armstrong, & Crosland (2009) and provided starting points for the Framework (Figure 5.1):

- Connect—Focus on relationships.
- Protect—Promote safety and trustworthiness.
- Respect—Engage in choice and collaboration.
- Redirect (Teach and Reinforce)—Encourage skill building and competence.

These principles align well with general classroom practice, and are intuitive for many teachers and educators but, until now, have had no education-specific application. The Framework uses these principles, applied through an educator's lens, to describe a learning space conducive to students learning to settle and expand.

Trauma-Responsive Guidelines

This Framework provides a set of recommendations and guidelines, based on best practices in trauma informed care, research into trauma and learning, and the work of other adult educators in this field. In particular, Schiffmann notes that trauma-informed structures put adult learners at ease "...because they are structures that help things run smoothly. They make explicit the processes participants can access to

---

Box 5.2 Definition of transactional relationships

Transactional relationships are built on the expectation of reciprocation. All parties are concerned with getting as much as they can, and bonds are broken the moment one party does not hold up their end.

For this reason, these relationships tend to be fragile and do not last (Transactional Relationships in Psychology: Definition & Examples, 2021).

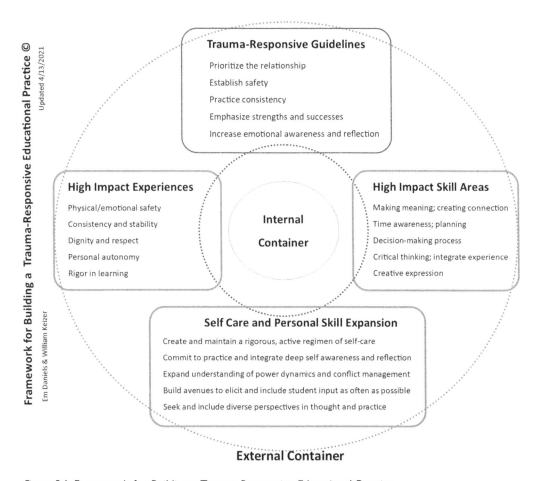

Figure 5.1 Framework for Building a Trauma-Responsive Educational Practice.

Source: Daniels, M and Keizer, W. (2020), Spokane WA. Copyright (2019) by M. Daniels. Reprinted with permission.

get their learning needs met....[creating] a shared understanding of *how* we do things in [the] classroom" (emphasis author's 2016).

Schiffmann also makes an important observation that trauma-responsive approaches "[r] equire us to be curious about the ways our students are experiencing learning..." (2016), a departure from traditional mental health approaches that tend toward educators understanding the trauma history, and adopting a therapeutic approach. In a trauma-responsive educational approach, we guide students in better understanding and rediscovering themselves as learners, strengthening their skills, and rebuilding their learning process.

The elements of the Framework, and classrooms described by Schiffmann, are intended to facilitate the state of deep, inner calm needed for expansive learning, and the instructor is pivotal in that facilitation. The deeper the state of inner calm of the instructor, the more easily they hold that state in the learning space. Menakem and van der

Kolk both tell us that physical proximity to settled nervous systems helps us settle, and maintain our own sense of calm. Students who have unsettled, hyper- or hypo-alert nervous systems may find a calm and settling environment uncomfortable at first. As they settle, they become more confident in their ability to learn, retain, and integrate that learning.

Operating from a trauma responsive perspective and shifting from "what's wrong with you?" to "what happened to you?" has the added benefit of emphasizing emotional objectivity. Calm and settled energy is as contagious as restless and distressed energy. The more you hold a sense of restful vitality, the more your students will grow accustomed to the experience, and seek and hold it also.

Prioritize the Relationship

Jones & Nichols (2013), Stevenson (2015), Ludy-Dobson and Perry (2010), and Menakem all talk about connection and proximity as necessary for trauma- and culturally responsive spaces. Prioritizing relationship has two direct connections to our work: First, trauma damages our ability to form connections with other people. We can relearn how to form those connections, in part, by experiencing healthy, well-defined relationships. Second, relationship and community are how many BIPOC students understand and interact with the world. Focusing on relationship, in addition to their achievements, acknowledges a different way of understanding the world by valuing and sharing that experience.

Prioritizing relationships in carceral spaces takes extraordinary care and awareness. Articulating the nature of relationship between teacher and student in any environment is challenging, and this is doubly true in carceral spaces, where the word "relationship" is always fraught with complexity and suspicion. In the context of extreme power dynamics, truly consensual relationships between those with power and those without are not possible, and that extends into the classroom.

Transactional relationships, where the authority figure and incarcerated person play their institutional roles, are considered necessary for "rehabilitation." These relationships are temporary, based on the exchange of authority and obedience. Authority cannot tolerate anything perceived as a challenge, so the relationships are fragile and inconsistent. Organized education also depends on this type of transactional, obedience-driven relationship, and can easily become an extension of corrections culture.

Relationships that acknowledge our shared, autonomous humanity are not the norm in organized education or in carceral spaces. Prioritizing the relationship requires we shift from the transactional and toward the relational. In prisons, that shift is limited, in part, because incarcerated people cannot truly give consent. Consent is foundational in mature, well-developed relationships and requires that people be able to withdraw that consent without fear of repercussion or retaliation.

Porges reinforces what we have learned—that trauma interrupts our ability to connect with others. His work reinforces the biological element when he notes, "Trauma disrupts the ability to relate to others and to use social behavior to literally regulate vagal function—to calm us down" (2014, p. 170). Connecting this to Menakem's work on settled systems influencing other settled systems, we can envision the following:

A settled person projects restful vitality, and holds their end of the relationship connection gently and firmly. This restful vitality is consistent. Regardless of how the person on the other end of the connection feels or behaves, they experience this steady, restful vitality from the settled person. Just as discordant, restless energy is contagious, so too is this restful vital energy. Staying focused on the relationship, regardless of circumstances, helps us maintain an unwavering connection and hold steady on our end of the relationship.

Prioritizing the relationship means you know where the trust and safety lines are and **you keep them there**, regardless of how your students respond. How they respond to your boundaries does not change that boundary, whether they want to come closer or move away. Your trust and safety line stays in the same place. When conflict arises (setting aside actual safety risks), your first thoughts need to be "How can I prioritize the relationship in this moment? How can I treat this person with dignity, no matter what is happening?"

Establish Safety

Safety is a tricky word, no matter the setting, and demanding students "feel safe" is problematic and harmful. Porges proposes a neurophysiological model of safety and trust that states "…safety is defined by feeling safe and not by removal of threat" (2014, pp. 23–24). Polyvagal theory, which arises from study of the autonomic nervous system and its role in our internal regulation process, points to certain muscle arrangements of the facial features, head, and neck, as well as throat and vocal chords that transmit settled/stimulated soundwaves, as providing cues for safety and (for individuals) feelings of safety. These arrangements are regulated on the unconscious level, and arise from our own feelings of internal settling and stability.

Porges' model further defines three conditions necessary for feeling safe:

1   The autonomic nervous system cannot be in a state that supports defense.
2   The social engagement system needs to be activated to down regulate sympathetic activation.
3   Detect cues of safety (e.g., certain types of vocalizations, positive facial expressions and gestures).

Early in my research I came across Dr. James Garbarino. He is considered an expert witness in cases where children are charged with murder and has interviewed over 100 people convicted as children of killing another person. In this brief paper, Garbarino notes that, on average, incarcerated people have an ACEs score of 6 or higher but that these child murderers average a score between 8 and 10 (2017).

Even though the ACE survey lists 10 horrifying experiences, it is not comprehensive. It is designed to survey only childhood experiences, does not include horrible things that happen to older adolescents and adults, nor can it take into account systemic or historic trauma, and how trauma compounds over a lifetime. It is limited in what it can tell us about students but what it CAN tell us is that students in carceral settings may never have experienced feeling safe, or may not be able to use those words while they're in prison. I propose that for harsh learning environments, we consider that *feeling safe* is secondary to the physical state of *being settled*.

Being settled and *feeling safe* are certainly connected and, ultimately, may even be the same thing. I chose the phrase "*being settled*" because people have influence over their physical state of being, regardless of how they may describe their feelings. "Safe," "safety," and "feeling safe" can be loaded words for people who have spent years in and out of systems, especially foster care and corrections. Throughout their lives, they hear those words over and over and over, as they are moved in and out of dangerous situations.

Giving students a way to describe their physical state without discussions of safety, or expectations that they feel safe, provides an alternative path toward internal calm. The phrase "be settled" removes the unspoken imperative to feel a certain way, and centers a state of being that students can practice.

Practice Consistency and Transparency

One of the reasons traumatic events are so devastating is that they happen unexpectedly and the event (or events) seem to be random, with no apparent cause. This portion of the traumatic experience reverberates on and on, as even minor disruptions keep people in a state of unease. Although they may not admit it, people benefit tremendously from at least a minimal routine and structure, including our students.

Experienced teachers know what happens when they do something unexpected, or change up a routine without notice: all our students are at least initially a bit shocked, and then they reorient and start asking questions. But there are always a few who cannot reorient without a great deal of reassurance and explanation, even then taking a while to resettle themselves. This is common behavior in adult classrooms and, like adult educators everywhere, I have had students who seem unable to adjust to the smallest change without a highly charged response.

Translating that experience into prison classrooms reveals competing sets of needs for students. Although they are very likely to feel high levels of anxiety and distress over unexpected changes, institutionalization and the power dynamic are at work making sure that they only express themselves in "appropriate" ways, if at all. Institutionalization, combined with prior educational trauma, can result in hypersensitive students who shut down or disassociate at the slightest hint of unease. Reactions to the unexpected may range from a flat affect to nervous jitters to an extreme version of respectful politeness, or polite aggression.

No matter how I describe it, it will come as a shock the first time you experience an abrupt and (seemingly) arbitrary change impacting your work. It can happen to you, to your students, your program, with no warning or explanation, and can be quite destabilizing. While you may not experience it often, it happens with regularity in your students' lives outside the classroom. All the unexplained changes in routine, expectations, and consequences disrupt feelings of safety, which is why **you** practicing consistency and transparency is so helpful.

Key to building trust and creating a calm, settled environment is being consistent and transparent in your behavior and decision making; students should be able to trust that you will react predictably, no matter the circumstances. As mutual trust grows, they will be more confident in expressing themselves and in adapting to unexpected events and changes.

Emphasize Strengths and Successes

Classroom culture rarely involves acknowledging each other in positive ways. We don't compliment or praise, and success is considered a personal endeavor, not a community effort. This maintains the illusion of the individual alone as important, and may reinforce disconnection from others as a "normal" state of being. Creating space for people to feel proud of themselves and others, simultaneously, fosters connection and healthy pride in achievement.

One of the first program changes I made when I was working inside was to add an Orientation. When I look back at those materials, I realize I was trying to accomplish an enormous number of tasks in a week's worth of hours. Orientation activities included establishing classroom culture, norms, and expectations, individual goal setting, personal development, teambuilding, fun and play activities, and basic skill building.

During orientation, one of our final activities, after all the students had gotten to know each other better, was to have a day of public acknowledgment. Each person would stand in front of the class and listen to a positive remark from every other student. I took notes, then made them a laminated copy we could put on the wall and share for the rest of the class. It was one of the most moving and transformational activities I've ever witnessed in a classroom, and it was not done lightly or without proper preparation.

Not everyone can or would want to facilitate such an activity, but there are many activities you can use to encourage your students to acknowledge each other. Positive interaction, giving and receiving, reduces fear by building confidence. Even if students don't necessarily believe everything good they hear about themselves, those positive reinforcements are still in their minds. Building confidence and competence is a contemporaneous process. Growth in one doesn't always mean growth in the other but they are closely connected.

Increase Emotional Awareness and Reflection

As mentioned earlier, you can help students increase their emotional awareness without public sharing. What matters most is that students become more aware of how they are feeling and can reflect on their internal state. Even a minimal increase in awareness can be helpful, especially when they are trying to understand themselves or get through difficult moments. Naming an emotion is a powerful tool for self-regulation, and students deserve all the tools we can give them.

No matter what you teach, you can do something to boost your student's emotional awareness. Almost every group I have ever been a part of has benefitted from a formal opening/closing activity as a way to focus and then reflect. You can give students a list of feeling words and ask them to check in with themselves every morning. Ask them to write themselves, or you, a little note, give them a few minutes to quiet themselves, followed with a short reflection—there are endless options.

The more you normalize emotional awareness and reflection, the more comfortable your students will become recognizing their own emotions. Keep in mind that this is a skill-building opportunity, not a therapeutic exercise, and you are not being asked to act in a therapeutic role. Helping students increase their awareness and vocabulary is good practice, and one of the ways learning spaces are beneficial in different ways than therapeutic spaces.

Containers

In any learning environment, the educator is responsible for creating and holding the container, or physiological, emotional, and spiritual space. Educators have greater and lesser degrees of control over the physical environment, but they have enormous influence over the invisible currents that shape their learning groups. Educational space needs to be constructed and held in a different manner than groups that convene to do facilitated work such as mediation, conflict management, or building other intentional spaces.

The teacher is the Internal Container in such spaces and, combined with the group (through norms, agreements, values, and accountability), provides the center for the External Container. Instructors, following the examples they've seen, prioritize content-related activity and discussion, using them to reinforce the container. Common classroom elements that often become proxy for a container include grading information (assignments, tests, homework, attendance), learning outcomes and materials, academic and conduct policies, and contact information. These elements are not unimportant, but teachers should control them, not vice versa. I have watched teachers needlessly escalate situations when they could not extricate themselves from demanding compliance with these details.

While techniques such as structured syllabi, visual organization, and safety plans can be employed by everyone, the trauma-responsive instructor actively works to expand and deepen their own state of internal calm and organization, giving themselves room for flexibility without sacrificing rigor. A balanced learning space considers content needs along with the learning and community needs of everyone in the learning space. Rigorous learning is enhanced when people feel settled, and strong containers are one aspect of a settled classroom.

Internal Container

Our Internal Container is our own center—the space that holds our mental, emotional, and spiritual selves, and it is mirrored in our External Container. We all have this center and it needs our care and attention. It is the aspect of ourselves we draw on when we are uncomfortable, confused, angry, and uncertain, and holds the knowledge, skills, experiences, and wisdom we have actively cultivated. It also contains any misinformation, weaknesses, gaps, and dirty pain we have neglected. The Internal Container needs to be flexible, comfortable with uncertainty, and well-seated.

Teaching is a form of facilitation and, like all facilitators, teachers are responsible for setting and maintaining the emotional tone of the group. The tone we set reflects our internal state whether we are unsettled and distressed, or calm and focused. When you step into a new way of teaching, you encounter new and different ways of learning, interacting, and relating with students. Your confidence and comfort with unexpected questions, conversations, and challenges sets the tone for your students' comfort and confidence. When you are unsettled, students sense and respond to that unease, no matter how well you think you are covering.

There is a close connection between the internal state and external presence of a person with a well-developed internal container. These people extend their own sense of internal calm outward as an additional support for people in their vicinity. Maintaining this state, regardless of external stimuli, builds trust and can inspire students to push themselves to do the same. As I settled internally, I was able to handle disruptions and conflicts in the classroom with more equanimity and less personal reactivity.

The Internal Container in the Framework is you. You are the authority figure, and the one responsible for holding the space, at least in the beginning. Depending on your circumstances, students may eventually become part of that holding, but it may take time. One of your priorities must be to do no further harm, and that requires dealing with your own dirty pain. Activated pain on your part is something students cannot safely avoid, and it can quickly retrigger their own unresolved issues. Even when they integrate themselves into the External Container, you hold the center.

Your internal container must include generosity. Generosity can only come from within, and may be the portion of the container students respond to most. Generosity of spirit is a vital ingredient in any group endeavor, but can only arise when we are generous with ourselves first. Our self-judgment, perfectionism, criticism, and black-and-white thinking will automatically reflect outward onto students until we learn generosity toward ourselves.

I have met so many educators who think that harshness in teaching is an indicator of care toward students. It always makes me sad to consider what their educational experience might have been, that they conflate kindness and generosity with weakness, and harshness with academic rigor and success. I have conflicting feelings about the "tough love" approach for exactly this reason: most of us have far too much experience with harshness, and far too little with generosity and care.

People, in general, respond to a generous spirit and, sometimes, it will kindle that openness and warmth in their own hearts. This is what I want for my students, that they feel accepted, valued, and cared for, regardless of the content they are tasked with learning.

External Container

The External Container is a combination of the infrastructure you bring (i.e., all the teaching and learning operational "stuff") and what you co-create with your students. Teachers who insist that their way is the only way create restrictive containers. It doesn't matter whether the teacher is extremely controlling or exerts no control at all; both are extremes and restrictive in their own ways. Containers that do not welcome mistakes do not welcome growth.

Trauma-responsive spaces should reflect a balanced approach that has room for movement in either direction. Sometimes the instructor needs to add structure, sometimes students need more freedom, and there is space for mistakes, accountability, and course-correction or change. As the authority figure, how you respond to mistakes and course-corrections determines how everyone responds. Normalize public accountability by being open to feedback and welcoming new ideas.

All teachers have preferences for how they like to conduct a classroom, and how they like things done. Shifting to a trauma-responsive practice asks you to align your preferences with the Guidelines, and adjust them to work in co-created spaces. Prioritizing the relationship with your students means that their needs are as important as yours and deserve equal consideration in terms of the External Container (pending any non-negotiable system requirements).

The External Container you create with your students should do the following:

1   Define classroom operations (including feedback and decision-making processes).
2   Set expectations for behavior and communication (group, student-student, and student-teacher).
3   Outline conflict management and disciplinary procedures.

These structures hold the potential to help students settle and move into expansive learning but *they are only beneficial if they are enforced consistently, at **all** times*. When students realize that you are serious and will uphold your shared agreements, they will settle into the structure and use it for guidance on their own. That experience of consistent and healthy structure helps students settle and feel confident in the group and environment.

High-Impact Components

The Framework identifies two distinct components for settling and expanding: High Impact Experiences and High Impact Skills. High Impact Experiences are environmental tools for settling, while Skills are personal tools for expansion. The items in these components are well-aligned to counterbalance some of the effects of trauma on learning, and most teachers already emphasize at least some of these skills and experiences. Reviewing these experiences and skills from a trauma-responsive perspective gives us greater insight into why they are helpful, and why so many of us use them instinctively.

These two components are compelling and unique aspects of education as a trauma-responsive practice, and demonstrate its necessity as a Point of Entry. Regardless of a person's access to or interest in deeper trauma healing and resolution, a trauma-responsive learning environment may make a lasting impression. The experiences and skills in the Framework are places to begin, in part because they are already so common in adult classrooms, but they present infinite space for creative growth.

Experiences

The Experiences components mirror the Trauma-Responsive Guidelines, emphasizing safety and stability, the value of the individual, and a rigorous approach to learning. High Impact experiences are those that help students experience and internalize being settled. Healthy, well-built Containers are an essential aspect of these experiences, as is maintaining high expectations for learning. You cannot control, or even know, exactly what students experience, but intention, observation, accountability, and reflection will help you monitor and adjust your impact.

PHYSICAL/EMOTIONAL SAFETY

Having early conversations about expectations, communication, feedback, and consequences is so important because having these things in place gives you a structure to work in when things get chaotic. You can go back to those early conversations and agreements, reminding yourself and students what you put in place for unsettled times, and hold both you and them accountable to those agreements. Every group will have a different set of agreements and there is a wealth of information on how to guide those conversations, so I have not included that information here.

I normally frame recommendations in a "do this" format, but in this case, a "Do not do" list is quite useful.

1   Don't make threats. Threats are an abuse of power and break trust immediately.
2   Don't set boundaries you can't or won't enforce. Not enforcing boundaries undermines credibility.
3   Don't ignore conflict. Normalize identifying uncomfortable or tense moments.
4   Don't make decisions in anger. Angry decisions feel like punishment, no matter the outcome.

It is not necessary to have a conversation about "safety" or even mention the word to your students. Integrating this list or your personal equivalent into your teaching practice is what matters, not whether your students know what you aren't doing.

CONSISTENCY AND STABILITY

How your students show up should not change how you show up. As the Internal Container, it is up to you to build a reputation for being consistent and stable. Students need to be able to trust that you will respond in the same manner, no matter what kind of issue or question arises. In any classroom, things can go sideways quickly, and restoring order after chaos can be a chore. The purpose of creating infrastructure and an External Container is to maintain stability when things get messy.

I have heard many times that an instructor is overwhelmed or frazzled, and doesn't have time to do things differently in the classroom. In free classrooms, students have other options for getting needs met if the instructor is having a hard time. They can access tutoring, the library, their friends and family, the Internet, other students, and the list goes on. In a prison classroom, the instructor is the main source (if not the only source) of information and support, so if the instructor is struggling, the students are likely also having a hard time.

Setting up your teaching and learning infrastructure will take some work, but you only have to do it once and it can go with you everywhere. Once it is defined, it requires much less work to maintain and adjust. Here are some pieces of my teaching and learning infrastructure:

1   No is always no, yes is always yes; students should feel confident that your answer would be the same no matter who asked.
2   Involve students in decision making; listen to and integrate their advice and feedback.
3   Articulate how you make decisions, including a timeline and follow-up.
4   Don't do for one what you can't do for all; consider outcomes before you respond to a request.
5   Surprises are unwelcome; give plenty of notice about upcoming changes in routine.

I developed these rules for myself years ago and I use them in every group situation I encounter, classroom or presentation hall.

DIGNITY AND RESPECT

Valuing a person's dignity and offering them respectful treatment matter greatly at all times, in all places. In systems designed to strip people of dignity and ignore their humanity, it is the role of a teacher to resist those efforts, and maintain a dignified and respectful learning space.

The phrase "treat people with dignity and respect" is used frequently in carceral spaces to describe how staff, in a systemic context, should treat incarcerated people. On the surface, the phrase describes a reasonable approach, but it takes little effort to reveal its coded nature. I have wondered many times how the words "dignity" and "respect" became conjoined in the carceral space context, and I suspect they have been assimilated into the coded language of the culture and system, much as the phrase "trauma-informed" is currently being assimilated.

I want to reiterate that I speak only from my experience, and from what I heard, observed, and witnessed. I cannot speak from the perspective of incarcerated people, or how they use and understand these terms. My hope is that you will take from this section that the dignity and respect you extend be genuine, consistent, and unconditional, not withdrawn if you perceive disobedience or a transgression against the system.

Explicitly treating people with dignity and showing respect is of such importance in a carceral space both because it is a best practice and because a true demonstration of these concepts is rare, despite frequent use of the phrase. In Chapter 4, I detailed the concealed tensions between education programs and work programs, describing underlying economic motivators. The hidden nature of the phrase "dignity and respect" requires a similar uncovering to grasp the importance of consciously extending respect and honoring dignity.

Respect and dignity are a starting point, even though they are co-opted by the system. It is possible for one person to be outwardly respectful to another as they take away property, lock shackles around wrists and ankles and belly, then watch that person shuffle into solitary confinement. It is possible that people walk into a room, strip, have their body handled without consent, and retain their dignity because dignity is internal and independent of external treatment.

Merriam-Webster defines *dignity* as "...the quality or state of being worthy, honored, or esteemed" (Dignity, 2021) and *respect* as "an act of giving particular attention" (Respect, n.d.). One is a state of being, the other is an action, an outward demonstration of attention. Dignity is internal, inherent to who we are. Respect is the way we treat others, and while it can provide a reasonable set of guidelines for interacting, may or may not arise from our internal state.

I dislike the word "respect" and find it a problematic linguistic shortcut for undefined behavioral and cultural expectations. The lack of explicit definition, shared understanding, and mutual agreement provides an extraordinary range of openings for misunderstanding, both unintentional and deliberate. For people who share similar cultures, norms, and backgrounds, there is more likely to be an understanding of what constitutes *respect*. In the United States, common indicators of *respect* include acknowledging authority; not challenging orders; using titles or honorifics; controlled body movement; low, quiet tone of voice; and asking for permission to speak.

None of these indicators are inherently wrong, but in carceral spaces, the Dominator dynamic restricts those expectations to one direction only: from incarcerated people toward prison/jail staff. The system demands that incarcerated people show proper *respect* to staff at all times, although the opposite is not true. In the same manner, *lack of respect* (an undefined phrase) can be linguistic shorthand for a range of behaviors, and a quick route to punishment. The ambiguity in these terms leads to constant, low-level friction, although the hidden definitions become more clear during conflict between incarcerated people and staff.

In those moments, *respect* reveals itself as a synonym for obedience and subservience. Corrections staff are trained to use the phrase "dignity and respect," but incarcerated people have no power to enforce dignified or respectful treatment. A system with genuine expectations of respect would require reciprocal behaviors, but true reciprocity is impossible in a system of domination. The only demands on system actors is that they comply with system requirements, and not in ways that could be proven to have broken rules or laws.

Dignity is of such value in trauma-responsive practice because it requires connection in order to acknowledge our shared humanity. Dignity cannot be bestowed, but can be recognized and protected. Dignity is the combination of our sense of self-worth and our belief in ourselves as fully human and deserving to be acknowledged as such. People with dignity may end up as targets in any system designed to dehumanize. Their belief in their own humanity reminds others—those who have dehumanized themselves—of the consequences of that dehumanization.

PERSONAL AUTONOMY

In spaces where people have no control over anything except their thoughts, recognizing, validating, and valuing personal autonomy is immensely important. Because all facilities are different, the amount of leeway you have in allowing students to make certain types of choices may be limited. You can ensure that they have plenty of opportunities to take control of and make choices about their learning process, even in the most constrained circumstances.

Choices that may seem small or irrelevant to you may matter a great deal to students, so create options whenever you can. Asking for and integrating their feedback about classroom processes, topics of discussion, homework deadlines, communication, activities—anything related to their learning—should be a class norm. **Do not give options if you cannot or will not honor their choices**. If you cannot allow a choice, it is better to say that up front than to give choices then ignore decisions.

RIGOR IN LEARNING

Do not misinterpret trauma-responsive teaching as less rigorous in its learning requirements. My entire academic career, as both a student and instructor, I have heard—explicitly and implicitly—that rigorous academics require harsh taskmasters. As someone who has an extensive transcript with coursework from more than half a dozen schools, my experience proved that truth in far too many instances. A trauma-responsive environment does not lessen rigor, but it does shift our thinking about learning requirements toward a balance between content expertise, cultural responsivity, and learning how to learn.

What IS safe to teach in carceral spaces? Much of the literature available on teaching in prison addresses that question and, specifically, how to teach specific types of content (e.g. Ginsburg (2019) andKarpowitz (2017)). These are necessary questions, especially for liberal arts instructors with a keen interest in developing critical thought using challenging materials, assignments, and ideas that might be viewed with suspicion in corrections classrooms. Harsh spaces require greater care with lesson planning, and adjustments for the lack of safety and privacy in students' daily lives.

From my own teaching, for example, I learned that I needed to have more care when I gave students topics for journaling. They have no privacy from security staff, and more than one student had their writing taken away and read, or discarded, by unit guards. Asking them to journal on sensitive topics may not only activate their pain, it may be compounded if their privacy is violated and those vulnerable writings are exposed. This does not mean you should not ask them to write and think and examine their experience, but that you help them learn how to do so in a way that both maintains rigor and reduces their potential exposure.

Balancing high expectations with consideration challenges our definitions of "poor" performance, as well as questioning whether that definition furthers Euro-white supremacist standards. I consider high expectations in terms of student effort—are students trying their hardest? What does progress look like for them? Are they pushing themselves to engage with content, as well as strengthening their ability to learn? The answers to those questions are different for every student, and evaluating them in the context of academic programming is not the easiest task.

Creating assessments that measure ability to learn as well as content expertise is an ongoing challenge for educators, and a difficult concept to measure in a system that values quantification, specificity, and defined outcomes above all else. Trauma-responsive practice, at its core, directly challenges the primacy of a system driven only by quantifiable outcomes, and that challenge presents a wealth of opportunity. In this place of harsh constraints, we are faced with the task of imagining how to equalize learning across the expansive learning elements, and redefining rigor in the context of the learning process.

Skills

Skills center on expanding the nervous system. Each item offers a counterbalance to a particular type of trauma impact—inability to connect or make meaning, disrupted time sense, emotional and reactive action, and contracted self-expression. Giving students a choice of skills to work on, defining their personal outcomes and measurements of success combines personal autonomy and rigor in learning. Skills lend themselves well to a holistic process that engages students in learning how to learn, and reflect on their own process. In this manner, students can take ownership of their learning.

Years ago I took a course on how to be a life coach. Even then, life coaching was considered a questionable occupation, not regulated or requiring any kind of true certification to practice. Coaching as an industry as grown, and that skepticism has grown with it, but the course I took was excellent and I use what I learned in every aspect of my teaching. Coaches are taught that people need to define their own goals and outcomes, but that often translates into the coach making suggestions, not the coachee finding their own definitions.

Truly giving people charge of their own learning—choosing where to focus, defining outcomes, setting goals—enormously increases the chances they will follow through and that they will remain committed lifelong learners. For experienced educators, letting someone with weak learner muscles choose their own path and then support them on that path is not easy. It is frustrating to watch them make mistakes, not push themselves enough, or flirt with quitting, and the temptation to step in can be overwhelming. If you are like me, you have stepped in once or twice and, to be kind, it did not go well.

Not stepping in and intervening is hard because we are conditioned to seek specific outcomes; outcomes that meet a certain standard or measure, that happen on a defined timeline, or are otherwise quantifiable. Our purpose in expansive learning and trauma-responsive practice is different, as we try to create more balanced learners and counteract the educational trauma suffered by so many of our students. We can do neither of those things within existing teaching paradigms, so we have to sit with the discomfort inside ourselves, and deal with our own anxiety about our teaching identity.

One of the most valuable teaching strategies I ever discovered, as mentioned earlier, was creating a classroom Orientation. One of its most useful purposes was to establish a shared set of basic skills and understandings. My students, for example, needed to learn basic keyboarding, how to visually organize and label assignments, and how to read and use the different elements of a textbook. I recommend you facilitate a series of skill-building activities and exercises for the entire group before ever starting with content. Let them know why are you are having them go through these exercises as a class, and listen to their feedback.

This introductory session should accomplish three things:

1   Instruct students in any processes they will have to do repeatedly, or that you require be done in a specific manner (anything from labeling homework to how to take good notes).
2   Allow you to evaluate individual skill levels.
3   Act as a community building exercise while establishing your expectations of group behavior and norms.

The educational aspect of this approach is secondary to treating students with dignity and increasing their confidence in themselves as learners. That impatience you feel when students aren't "getting it" is your work to address. When I find myself growing impatient, it is most often rooted in feeling frustrated that I haven't explained a concept clearly enough, or that I am somehow not teaching correctly. When you find yourself in an agitated state during teaching, take a moment and consider what you can do to increase your students' confidence—right then—even though you feel terrible. Put aside your own need to vent your frustration and find something they are doing right; find a way to connect with them as learners and as people.

We are all from a system that rushed and forced our learning process. We were not allowed to take the time and space we needed to explore ourselves as learners, so we have few models for this type of approach. You set the tone for learning, even if you are venturing into the unknown. Making the commitment to enjoy the learning itself, with all its messiness and discomfort, gives your students permission to do the same.

MAKING MEANING; CREATING CONNECTION

When our ability to make meaning of things that happen is short-circuited, we experience the world as a series of disconnected and random events that just … happen. We cannot place them in relation to ourselves, our actions, or the actions of others. We live in a whirlpool, tossed about and spiraling up or down on a whim. Meaning making and creating connection are closely linked, so our ability to connect with others is also disrupted, creating a profound sense of isolation as we attempt to navigate a seemingly meaningless series of events.

Fortunately, meaning-making and creating connection are skills that can be learned, re-learned, and re-created. This can happen in a variety of ways, and learning spaces provide a wide span of opportunity. Key to this relearning is talking with students up front about meaning-making and why it matters. Beginning with an exploration of why learning matters, why it should matter to them, and how education exists within the larger scope of learning can give them both an example and a model for inquiry. Guide students to explore what learning and education mean to them, then connect with each other around this exploration. This activity provides a rich repository of shared meaning they can draw from throughout your time together. Teach them how to reflect on their experiences in learning, then share with each other as part of the full cycle of knowing themselves as learners.

Having this conversation before you start any type of content or program is a major departure from organized education classrooms, and both you and students may flail around a bit. That is to be expected, and flailing around together is a good way to create connection as well as co-discover meaning in your shared experience. It will feel unfamiliar and likely trigger your desire to exert authority and get things "back on track." At some point, you may need to do this, but try to trust the process and give it room to breathe and expand.

Remember that you are on this journey with them, and that you will likely make mistakes. Including that in the conversation—that you are as accountable to them as they are to you—means that you have to acknowledge when it is hard for you to relinquish control over the learning process. But part of this work is challenging profound isolation and separation, and being together in learning is one way to meet that challenge.

TIME AWARENESS AND PLANNING

Teaching students some version of time management is standard in any classroom. Teachers think students do not manage time well, and students think teachers demand too much of their time. In prisons, students do have more time to work outside of the classroom, but time management can still be an issue. In my experiences, however, I do not think time management is an accurate phrase. Cultures interact with time differently, and our concept of time management is based in the Euro-white cultural perception of time.

There is extensive research into the influence of trauma on time awareness. Trauma researchers investigate how trauma interrupts our perceptions, causing flashbacks, traumatic amnesia, dissociation, all of which contribute to time distortions. Prison life and institutionalization contribute to distorted time perception and weaken students' ability to correctly estimate how much time they need to accomplish goals and complete tasks.

Time awareness is easy to teach because it is concrete and your students understand its importance. Where I saw students run into trouble was taking tests (partially an artifact of educational trauma), underestimating the time needed for complex projects (in or out of the classroom), and planning for the future. The latter two are connected in that students would have a vision but could not put together a realistic plan to bring their vision into being. Some students, especially those who came from violent and chaotic backgrounds, could not envision beyond a week or month in the future. They had no expectation of survival, so why dream for the future?

I know that working with students on this skill in particular can be infinitely frustrating. It is hard to comprehend how some students continually struggle but remember—you don't know what's happening in their brain, or how they perceive time. Set small, easy goals for as long as it takes and check in with them often. Anytime they reach a goal, make sure to acknowledge their success. If you know there is a big assignment coming up, take time to work with them and map out each step. Have them report in frequently with a progress update. You may only have to do this once or twice for them to learn, but do not abandon them after a success. Check in occasionally, just to make sure overconfidence has not taken command.

Common teaching practice for big projects is to schedule checkpoints that include specific goals and tasks for the entire class. I made a practice of checking in with students at least once before the first checkpoint and if they were having trouble, immediately helping them map out smaller steps. This will feel like micro-management at first but for some students, it is the level of guidance they need to help them learn. But do not forget to stop micro-managing and give them space to wobble around. They may have setbacks, but those setbacks won't have the same amount of stopping power as before.

Your students' perception of time might not change, but they will be more aware of their own time-related needs with regard to learning. Having them create a structured plan with a timeline and small, easy goals is excellent practice for managing everything that will be required of them as they return to the community and afterward. Structure and organization also help them manage information, control their thinking, and make decisions, another point of interdependence across skills.

DECISION-MAKING PROCESS

I had a student who was constantly getting into small scrapes and arguments with the guards in the dorm. In order to stay in the program, students had to maintain good behavior in all aspects of their lives, so ongoing problems with bunkmates and guards was concerning. When I asked why the student continued to engage in the same activities, they said they didn't know. When I asked about their decision-making process, how they were coming to the decision to interact, the student's face went blank.

This student did not realize that each engagement, each interaction, was the result of decisions they were making. They did not realize they even had a decision-making process, but thought they had to react immediately to anything that happened. When I explained that the process was happening, even if they didn't recognize it or it was happening unconsciously, they were stunned.

The first step in them recognizing their decision-making process was to answer all questions, for a 24-hour period, with "I need to think about that, I'll get back to you," go to their bunk and think about the question for 15 minutes, and then give an answer. At this time, we didn't worry about the decisions themselves, only about bringing the process into consciousness, and getting the student familiar with its presence.

Students will have different levels of experience with decision making, and it is always good practice to go through the steps together. Even people with high-level skills can use a refresher, and it will help everyone understand your expectations. Never assume that people make decisions the same way; focus on teaching them to understand and describe their own process rather than forcing them to follow a particular set of steps. Students who are unfamiliar with making decisions consciously may need to use a defined set of steps in the beginning, but encourage them to explore defining their own process.

As students learn to step through and describe their process, talking about how to slow down decision making is crucial. In the *7 Habits of Highly Effective People* (2004), Covey talks about extending the time between stimulus and response. In all my work with students, this may be the skill that had the most immediate impact. Many of the people I've taught had never realized they could take time to think before making decisions or taking action, so they simply reacted in the moment. Once they understood that they could exercise control over their own process, we saw remarkable shifts.

Many of the choices that show up in our lives are out of our control. What we can control is how we make decisions and how we learn from the result of those decisions. Understanding that we can control how we make decisions, even if the choices and outcomes are not what we want, can give meaning to what otherwise feels arbitrary. Giving students choices as much as possible is feeding two birds with one hand—they experience themselves as autonomous and get to practice making decisions.

CRITICAL THINKING; INTEGRATE EXPERIENCE

Critical thinking is heavily emphasized in most classrooms, although I am not certain any two teachers would have the same definition! In a trauma-responsive classroom, critical thinking must be linked with both information and lived experience. In its role as a high-impact skill, teaching students to think critically combines meaning-making with content knowledge. I hear constantly that students struggle with critical thinking but I think what many instructors miss is making a concrete connection to a student's lived experience.

Even for the strongest learners, new or abstract ideas can be difficult to absorb both in terms of information and making some connection within their own understanding. Imagine the confusion and fear for someone with a significant trauma history—all the skills and connections needed to take in and realize something new may be weak or barely there. Seeking out and praising every success, no matter how small, is the way to increase their confidence and strengthen those weak pathways. Acknowledging their work publicly, with permission and as appropriate, can also be rewarding for them and everyone who has been cheering them along.

CREATIVE EXPRESSION

Almost every form of creative expression is used to counteract the impacts of trauma, and for the sheer joy of self-expression. Humans are naturally creative, and expression of that creative self is enormously beneficial. Even if you do not have much time, giving students time for creative activity whenever possible can help them find their place of internal calm, preparing them for learning. I recommend that any classroom make space for creative expression and encourage all students to participate in some way.

Prisons often have a stationary program where imprisoned artists create work that is used on stationary sold only to other incarcerated people. While I was teaching inside, the prison stationary program was embedded in my larger program, so I oversaw between four and six artists who submitted art weekly. I learned that most of them had not been artists before they came to prison, and had never even thought of themselves as artists.

Art in prisons is not a new concept, and there are art programs scattered in prisons around the country. The Alabama Prison Arts & Education (APAE) project has been in place since 2003 and is one of the longer-running programs in the country. According to the history from their website,

> ...The goals of APAEP have always been to place rich creative and intellectual opportunities in Alabama's prisons, a remarkably underserved population....APAEP grew from one poet teaching in one prison, to a pool of more than 100 writers, artists, scholars, and visiting writers teaching in twelve correctional facilities in Alabama. Course offerings have grown from poetry to a wide variety of courses in the arts and humanities. ..." (2021)

One of the saddest by-products of educational trauma is hearing a student say "I'm not creative," or "I'm not an artist," knowing that the stories behind those beliefs are routinely terrible. Combining creative expression with academic learning gives students additional choices in exercising autonomy, helping themselves settle into learning, and building confidence in themselves as expressive, expansive people.

The Framework demonstrates the interdependence of each of the elements. Skills and experiences inform and define each other, but are reliant on strong Internal and External containers to be at their fullest. We want students to feel capable and competent both academically and as connected learners, guided, in part, by what their teacher models for them. The teacher provides the example, and guides students into creating community and holding space for each other. In all of this, the educator's presence and confidence are pivotal. They are the difference in a learning space that replicates trauma cycles and structures of oppression, or one that presents students with choice, autonomy, and a celebration of their full, creative humanity.

Self-Care and Personal Skill Expansion

This component of the Framework is located at the bottom of the Container circles to indicate that it is both grounding and foundational to a trauma-responsive practice. It is impossible to overstate the need for a rigorous regime of self-care in order to maintain well-being in the face of consistent injustice and ongoing harm to others. Tending our health requires dedication to our own regenerative practice, practicing settling, and releasing our dirty pain.

In conversations about self-care, the first thing I hear people mention are hobbies and recreational activities. The conversation rarely ventures beyond those surfaces, into the more delicate territory of deeper health, wellness, and balance. Organizers and activists are on the leading edge of this work; how we care for ourselves and each other under immense pressure and inside of structures designed to crush and oppress. BIPOC people, especially women, are consistently pressured into caregiving roles, and stereotyped as "strong," to their detriment and continual exhaustion.

The drive to be "ok," not show our vulnerability, or appear weak is so deeply ingrained in our psyches that it operates like a protective reflex. We dismiss questions and concerns, refusing to connect and share our vulnerable hearts, without realizing what we have done or why. We don't know how to talk with each other about caring for ourselves, often viewing such care as selfish, self-serving, and unnecessary.

If you do not learn to identify and care for your own needs, you put yourself (and your students) at risk as someone who looks to their students for emotional support and validation. Your reservoir of unacknowledged dirty pain will eventually leak onto your students, continuing the cycles of harm for you and for them. Lack of self-knowledge and self-awareness is particularly problematic in corrections classrooms where relationships with students are under constant scrutiny.

There is grace in every step we take toward becoming our best selves, no matter our starting point. What we cannot do is ask others to do work we are unwilling to undertake. As we enhance our understanding of trauma and strive to create trauma-responsive learning spaces and personal practice, we must also address our own turmoil and pain. Committing to an internal practice, whatever form it takes, keeps us aligned with our expectations in classroom and elsewhere.

Create and Maintain a Routine

Just as creating a classroom routine is good for your students, creating a personal routine is good for you. Structure matters more than we realize, especially when we are tired, depressed, and not thinking clearly. Establishing a routine when we are feeling nourished, vibrant, and clear-headed keeps us aligned with what we need in order to maintain that state of being. We have all had those moments of feeling terrible and trying to decide what we needed in order to feel better, when it seemed nothing would help us feel better. It is infinitely harder to find our way back to well-being without a trail of personal breadcrumbs.

Also true is that we do not always recognize when we are feeling well, or even less bad. Disconnecting from our own pain and suffering also disconnects us from feeling our wellness and vitality. Reconnection, on every level, is a non-linear process that is the work of our lifetimes. So many times I have reconnected to myself and thought, "Well, that was hard and I'm so glad it's finished!" only to run up against the same issue again and again.

Our pain is literally embodied in our flesh and mind and heart and spirit, but we are made of much more than our suffering. Create a structure for yourself by noticing the times when you do feel well and what led to that feeling, committing to practices that nourish all the aspects of your being, and keep this information in a central place, where you can turn to your more vital self for direction and guidance. As you practice, taking care of yourself will become a habit.

Personal Skill Development

During the time I was teaching in prison, I found I needed an even more extensive repertoire of teaching tricks to handle the complex blocks to learning I encountered. I did extensive research into personalities, learning styles, impacts of poverty, addictive and criminal behaviors, human development and psychology, power dynamics, the cycle of abuse and violence, boundary setting, and anything else I could think of that would help me better teach my students how to learn and, more importantly, how to learn as a community—in relationship.

My background in communication, writing, art, conflict resolution, peace studies, and education served me well. A wide range of experience in technology, business, and higher education (and colleges in general), as well as an incredibly varied employment history gave me a breadth of experience that gave us many paths to connection. I worked some of the same jobs they had, or in the same industries, and had real-world experience using what I was teaching.

I did not know any other corrections educators interested in learning the way I was, and educators on free campuses did not understand the culture and environment. I organized everything as best I could, but what I didn't have was a way to evaluate and organize what I'd learned. I couldn't find a comprehensive framework that brought these disparate pieces into a coherent whole. There were things I knew worked, but I didn't know why and I wasn't sure if I could replicate them anywhere else. I kept doing them because I saw my students changing and growing in confidence, but the only reason I could give was "because it feels right."

I pursued learning as much as I could and continued developing my personal skill set partly because there was no information on what worked, why it worked, and what that meant in the longer arc of my students' lives. As I listened to my students prepare to release, I started learning about the obstacles facing them upon reentry and realized there was a whole other set of considerations that needed to be addressed. At that time, there was even less information about reentry than there was about teaching inside, so I started developing presentations on how to best advise students with conviction histories who wanted to return to school.

I share these pieces of my experience to demonstrate that there is no one combination of skills, training, degree, or employment history that will prepare you for teaching in general, or teaching inside in particular. That said, there is a basic skillset that I think all teachers should have, inside or outside, that has proven endlessly useful.

DE-ESCALATION AND CONFLICT MANAGEMENT

I have witnessed my share of tense moments in and out of correctional facilities. The thread through most of them is that if the person in the authority position had not allowed themselves to escalate, the situation would have gone in a different direction. Of course, being aware of our own escalation is closely linked to awareness of our own triggers and unresolved pain, but de-escalating is also a set of skills you can use even if you are having intense feelings.

I don't think there is a more valuable set of skills for anyone who works in helping professions than de-escalation and conflict management. Corrections training may include something called de-escalation, but it is taught as a technique for control, not for prioritizing relationship or valuing an individual's autonomy. Trauma-responsive de-escalation will do both, even if the outcome is the same. There will be times you have to enact disciplinary measures, but you can respect your students' autonomy and preserve their dignity.

IMPROVISATION AND HANDLING THE UNEXPECTED

Improvisation (improv) is the art and practice of dealing with the unexpected in any situation. It is commonly known as a theater and performance art, but Applied Improvisation brings the tools of improv into non-performance settings, such as teaching and workplace interaction. Addressing and challenging our positionality and authority as content experts is hard, but improv provides a way to explore our vulnerability in lower-risk environments. Improv holds a rich and well-developed set of tools, which means we walk into the classroom with options on responding to the unexpected.

COMMUNICATION

Read and study as much as you can about communication styles, group and individual dynamics, written, verbal and nonverbal cues, and cultural similarities and differences. A broad understanding of communication will help with conflict management, especially at the group level. This section is quite short as there is a wealth of information available, and everyone's communication needs and interests are quite different.

FACILITATION

Facilitation is the art and skill of holding the container for a group by managing and tracking the flow of conversation, communication, ideas, and resources. It is a practical, though underrated skill, and one that all adult educators should learn. I have watched many classroom discussions that were less engaging and led to confusion and misunderstanding, in part because the educator was an inexperienced facilitator.

Classroom discussions are conversations, even if they have defined topics and structure, and good conversation doesn't happen by accident. A skilled facilitator makes conversation seem effortless and fluid, keeps the group energy moving, watches individual engagement, addresses potential conflict or points of tension, and may tend to details like taking notes and keeping a parking lot of ideas. This level of facilitation comes, in part, through years of practice, but you do not have to learn on the fly or reinvent the wheel. If you have never had facilitation training, put it on your skill development list.

SETTING AND HOLDING BOUNDARIES

Setting and holding boundaries is a skill we all need to learn. No one is born knowing what to do, we learn from watching the people around us and personal experience. This is an unfortunate way to learn such an important set of skills, as most people have learned poor boundary management. When you have spent your life with weak or nonexistent boundaries, setting and enforcing them for the first time can be uncomfortable.

A friend once compared holding even the mildest boundary for the first time to feeling like they had erected a brick wall, and I agreed. Setting and holding boundaries can be a difficult task, even for people with strong boundary management practices. The earlier section on "Consistency as a High-Impact Experience" has examples to help you decide your personal and classroom boundaries.

If you need something specific to prison classrooms, consider setting up a rule to complement your boundary. Students generally test boundaries, but not maintaining your boundaries in a carceral setting carries the risk of severe consequences for you and them. For example, a rule in my classroom was that students could use the printer for class-related things (résumés, cover letters, certain assignments) as long as they were enrolled in the program. Once they were finished, however, they no longer had that access. In prison, giving access to some students (based on our past history) and not others would be considered "special treatment," and carried a number of consequences.

A former student came to me and asked to print a résumé. Even though I liked the student and certainly wanted to help, I could not. It would have been easy to do, and maybe no one would ever have known, but more likely is that other former students would have found out and come to ask for the same favor. This would have put me in the position of either giving one student special treatment and telling everyone else "no," or saying "yes" to everyone, although that would violate constraints on the Education department. Using the program rule to enforce a consistent boundary was unpleasant, but only had to be done once. Boundary management is well worth the time effort it takes to learn and integrate.

Self-awareness and Reflection

We have discussed the need for self-awareness and reflection a great deal already, so this section is short. First, keep your emotional needs out of the classroom. You are not there to receive emotional support and validation from your students, nor are you there to create an unbounded emotional release space. This a toxic and co-dependent dynamic that will undermine your credibility and effectiveness, and may put you in a position to manipulate or be manipulated.

Emotional manipulation is a phrase you will hear frequently in DOC training, and is a complicated topic for trauma-responsive educators. Part of our work is to prioritize healthy relationships with students but we all come into the work at different points on our own emotional journeys. Working in carceral spaces means that all relationships are under scrutiny and will be met with suspicion, no matter how healthy, transparent, and well defined. In a place of such skewed power dynamics, it takes time and practice to get a sense of what is and is not "normal."

Second, and this is a delicate topic, pay attention to how you are soothing yourself. People in corrections, especially security staff, have high rates of substance use, domestic violence, are more likely to commit suicide, and die early (Smith & Centers, 2020). Sixty percent of incarcerated people meet the criteria for a substance use disorder, while another 25%, although not meeting that criteria, were under the influence of a substance at the time off their arrest (National Institutes of Health, n.d.).

You are working in a space where symptoms of trauma exposure are ubiquitous, but talking about or even acknowledging these symptoms, their cause, and their impacts is taboo. I once heard a corrections employee say that every day, on the drive home, they looked for a certain mile marker. Once they passed that marker, they locked away everything that happened that day, so they wouldn't think about it once they were home.

I have never forgotten that story or its implications.

I cannot overstress the importance of self-accountability, debriefing after difficult interactions, and talking with colleagues regularly. I strongly recommend a type of therapy that works for you and that is culturally healthy, as well as plenty of rest, hydration, and a balanced diet. When you are feeling depressed or upset about work, do not give in to the tendency to isolate—reach out and let your community support you. Hard days and times are inevitable, but training and awareness will help. If you are taking rigorous care of yourself, your chances of engaging in self-destructive behavior are less, although it will take time to determine exactly what works for you.

Including Student Feedback

I included this in the Personal Skill Expansion piece of this component because even reading student feedback can be an upsetting experience for educators. Reading and hearing that we are not the educators we think we are can feel like a personal attack on our expertise and identity, and a challenge to our authority in the classroom. Being asked to integrate that feedback can feel even more invasive and uncomfortable—an even stronger challenge to our identity as a content expert and skilled practitioner.

If you can convince yourself to stand down and seriously consider your students' ideas, they will make you a better teacher. I recommend building a feedback component into your classroom structure, and giving your students a tutorial on how to give helpful feedback.

Even if they have some experience offering their thoughts and opinions, I found that giving them a structured way to comment helped them clarify their thinking.

However you decide to take feedback, make sure the process includes a timeline for your response and meet that timeline. If you decide to integrate student ideas, be sure to let them know and give them public credit (if they want public credit). Even if an idea seems out-rageous, if it is interesting, run it by your colleagues and/or supervisor and see if it is possible. When you are new to the environment, it takes a while to develop a sense of what you can make happen.

Seeking Diverse Perspectives

Whatever you are teaching, talk to as many people as you can get to talk with you about both content and process, whether they have experience teaching in prisons and jails or not. You may not be able to change your content or curriculum, but there are always places where you can include a new voice, or different ways you can present information. This is certainly more work for you, but will serve your students well—especially if you include the voices of system-impacted people, BIPOC, and disabled communities. Representation matters, and it matters even more in spaces where people have had few role models who look like them, or share their lived experience.

Accountability and Generosity

Accountability is a theme throughout the Framework, even though it is not specifically named. Many of the lingering impacts of trauma are connected to a broken or missing chain of accountability. No one admits what happened, how much it hurt, who did it, why they did it, or that it happened at all. Mutual accountability with your students is key to main-taining an expansive learning space.

Accountability is another word that has a layered meaning in corrections environment. On the surface, even the word "corrections" is about accountability and rehabilitation but as we have seen, the surface does not hold the entire story. The common definition of *accountability* is being willing to accept responsibility for your actions, which is reasonable much of the time. *Accountability* is problematic in corrections in the same way that *respect* is problematic: enforcement is inconsistent and usually applied only to incarcerated people.

While some corrections staff might be satisfied with someone acknowledging a mistake (or *taking accountability*), others might decide to administer *consequences* (i.e., punishment) and others might go as far as formal disciplinary measures. Mistakes made by corrections staff, however, are not treated in the same way, and incarcerated people have few options to demand accountability. Their avenues are limited to what the system allows, and the threat of punishment (formal or informal) is always present.

A trauma-responsive classroom requires accountability, but you need to be clear that accountability goes in both directions. Just as you expect students to be responsible for their mistakes, you will be responsible for yours. While not listed in either component, learning to give each other the benefit of the doubt, and assuming the best is a crucial aspect in both Experiences and Skills.

I found myself learning to be more generous as I worked with students and understood more what they needed and, in turn, I watched them become more generous with them-selves and each other. You play a key role by being both generous of spirit and modeling generous action, knowing that your students will take their examples from you. How you treat them is how they will treat each other, and people elsewhere in their lives.

No, You Can't Ask

We have all hurt students, replicating the harm done to us, either through our participation in the systemic oppression and racism perpetuated by organized education, personal malice or dislike, frustration and irritation, or simple ignorance. Details about traumatic events and circumstances are rarely useful in educational contexts, but what IS useful is accepting that adult students come to us with complex and multi-layered histories, including educational trauma. Accepting this about our students, without needing or searching for details, frees us up to focus on helping them reclaim themselves as learners.

Acknowledging this truth is a critical step in our growth as people and as educators. Arguing about our intentions is useless and ineffective if we are interested in change. Our best path forward is to accept what has happened, address our ignorance, and integrate that new awareness into our educational praxis.

Asynchronous and Remote Learning

With the rise of online, asynchronous, and remote learning, the question of how to build a trauma-responsive practice with little in person instruction becomes more urgent. Conversations with dozens of other prison educators produced a wealth of suggestions, and there are many exceptional, talented, and experienced educators who are leading this work. Building a classroom container of any kind in a correspondence or remote environment presents serious challenges, but it is not impossible.

* Set ground rules and expectations similar to those in a face to face class
* Include information about who you are as a teacher and your teaching philosophy
* Use best practice design elements such as Universal Design for Learning (UDL), Accessible Education, and Transparency in Teaching and Learning (TiLT) to address accessibility concerns.

Those of us teaching now, even newer teachers and those still finishing school, have had almost an entirely face-to-face learning experience, and even with online classes, the majority of students prefer in-person learning. That will not always be the case and when prisons and jails decide to adopt online and remote learning, we need to be ready. The reinstatement of Second Chance Pell means that education in prison could be on the road to a resurgence, and increased remote learning is on the way.

Despite the challenges, there are students who benefit greatly from this mode of learning—introverts and those who like more time to consider and turn over ideas may be quite pleased. Pressing through your discomfort or unhappiness with an unfamiliar teaching modality is your work, and must not be neglected.

The Most Radical Act

In a system designed to dehumanize, it is a radical act to acknowledge and celebrate our shared humanity. Teachers in these systems can extend that radicalism by building a joyful community of learners; of people discovering and rediscovering their love of learning and curiosity about the world. Prison classrooms, stripped of most material teaching aids, drive us to reimagine both teaching and learning.

With time, the prison environment and constrictions become less relevant. I shared them with you so you can walk in with some preparation but don't get distracted and let them become the focus. You can't forget where you are, but you cannot allow your circumstances to dictate the level of joyful learning you share with your students. Your students are the single most important concern—always. If you are thrilled about learning—especially about *their* learning—they will be too.

I was never told that teaching adult students could be a celebration and an act of joy. My colleagues and I spent less time imagining and dreaming about what education and learning *could be*, and more time trying to make our way through its bureaucratic reality.

This is upside-down thinking.

Although, like generosity, the Framework doesn't include imagination, a vigorous, lively imagination is an essential piece of a trauma-responsive practice. Your comfort level with imagining and exploring new ideas sets the tone for students to explore and dream—let them imagine with you, and delight in learning together.

Pursuing Imagination

Visioning, joy, and imagination matter greatly in places of harshness and inhumanity. The more you imagine and dream, the more chances you have of recognizing an unusual circumstance or opportunity to change the how and what of learning. The more pathways to the lightbulb moments you will forge or uncover. Give yourself permission to imagine teaching and learning as glorious experiment after glorious experiment. You won't use most of what you dream, but the dreaming itself is what matters; it keeps you open to wonder and, as noted by the late, beloved Sir Terry Pratchett, when that particle of raw inspiration sleets through the universe and into your head, you'll be waiting for it (Pratchett, 1996).

Adult educators need

- Permission to imagine and dream again; to seek delight in their imaginations.
- Immersion in expansive learning and the full experience of joy in their own learning.

I have been searching for this book for almost two decades. I knew, when I was in grad school, that there was something else I was trying to say—to find—but it stayed hidden because my imagination wasn't strong enough yet. I love learning, so I kept at it, practicing, strengthening my imagination, opening it wider. When Bill and I began working together, the last pieces fell into place and I imagined the Framework and felt its implications.

As I wrote, I realized there wasn't a way (that I could find) to talk about what I was trying to express, so I imagined the Points of Entry, then the Expansive Learning Model (Chapter 6!). None of these ideas emerged solely from wishful daydreams – they are the result of thousands of hours of teaching, researching, conversation, heartbreak, dismay, joy, and celebration; of thousands of hours spent dreaming and imagining new ways to help all students; of how education and learning shape so much of who we are and the world we have made.

References

Covey, S. R. (2004). *The 7 habits of highly effective people: Restoring the character ethic*. New York, NY: Free Press.

Dignity (2021). Retrieved from https://www.merriam-webster.com/dictionary/dignity

Garbarino J. (2017). ACEs in the criminal justice system. *Academic Pediatrics*, 17(7), 32–33. doi:10.1016/j.acap.2016.09.003

Ginsburg, R. (Ed.), (2019). *Critical perspectives on teaching in prison.* New York, NY: Routledge.

hooks, b. (2001). *All about love.* New York, NY: Harper Collins.

Hummer, V., Dollard, N., Robst, J., Armstrong, M., & Crosland, K. (2009). Innovations in implementation of trauma-informed care practices in youth residential treatment: A curriculum for organizational change. *Child Welfare, 89*(2), 79–95.

Jones, B., Nichols, E. (2013). *Cultural competence in America's schools.* Charlotte, NC: Information Age Publishing.

Kaba, M. (2021). *We do this 'til we free us: Abolitionist organizing and transforming justice (Abolitionist Papers).* Chicago, IL: Haymarket Books.

Karpowitz, D. (2017). *College in prison: Reading in an age of mass incarceration.* New Brunswick, NJ: Rutgers University Press.

Ludy-Dobson, C.R., & Perry, B.D. (2010). The role of healthy relational interactions in buffering the impact of childhood trauma. In E. Gil (Ed.), *Working with children to heal interpersonal trauma: The power of play* (pp. 26–43). The Guilford Press.

National Institutes of Health. (n.d.). *Criminal justice drug facts.* Retrieved from https://www.drugabuse.gov/publications/drugfacts/criminal-justice

Porges, S.W. (2014). *Clinical insights from the polyvagal theory: The transformative power of feeling safe. (Norton series on interpersonal neurobiology).* New York, NY: W. W. Norton.

Pratchett, T. (1996). *Wyrd sisters.* New York, NY: Orion Publishing Group, Limited.

Respect. (n.d.). Retrieved from https://www.merriam-webster.com/dictionary/respect

Schiffmann, T. (2016). *How trauma impacts the brain of the adult learner.* Retrieved from http://www.tracyschiffmann.com/blog/2016/11/4/how-trauma-impacts-the-brain-of-adult-learners

Schiffmann, T. (2016). *Make your classroom safe for trauma-impacted adult learners.* Retrieved from http://www.tracyschiffmann.com/blog/2016/11/4/make-your-classroom-safe-for-trauma-impacted-adult-learners

Smith C., & Centers, G. R. (2020). *Substance use and addiction among corrections officers.* Retrieved from https://www.graniterecoverycenters.com/resources/substance-use-and-addiction-among-corrections-officers/

Stevenson, B. (2015). *Just mercy.* New York, NY: One World/Ballantine.

The Alabama Prison Arts + Education Project. (2021). *History.* Retrieved from http://apaep.auburn.edu/history/

Transactional relationships in psychology: Definition & examples. (2021). Retrieved from https://study.com/academy/lesson/transactional-relationships-in-psychology-definition-examples.html

van der Kolk, B. (2014). The body keeps the score. New York, NY: Penguin Books.

Wartenweiler, T. (2017). Trauma-informed education: An interpretative phenomenological analysis. *The Online Journal of New Horizons in Education, 7*(2), 96–106.

Chapter 6

Learning, Growth, and Evolution

How we learn is a reflection of how we experience the world. How we experience the world is infinitely complex, and everchanging, but our ability to learn, grow, and change underpins and shapes that experience. When our ability to learn is compromised or harmed, that underpinning is weakened. We are less open, less willing to adapt and be flexible, or even believe ourselves as capable, competent learners. We may stop learning altogether, shut down our curiosity about the world, and box ourselves into our daily routines, rarely thinking about who and what exists outside of our immediate environment.

When we are challenged to think more broadly, consider new ideas, and face a rapidly changing world, our lack of confidence in ourselves as learners surges forward. The surge of fear is powerful, confusing, and overwhelming, and we want whatever is causing us such distress to stop, to leave us in peace. This is our activated fear response and its job is to protect us, to ensure we survive. It doesn't care that the threat may not be real, it cares that it feels real. As long as that fear response is awake and in defense mode, our nervous system is contracted—much like a sea anemone that contracts at even the lightest touch.

While the nervous system is agitated and contracted, the brain and body thrum with stress chemicals, slowing down and weakening the connection to our learning centers. Our nervous system cannot relax and settle, or bring us to the state of internal calm necessary for learning and integration. Long-term stress results in toxic chemical buildup, physical stagnation, and a reluctance to freely expand in any capacity—movement, rhythm, speech, or connection with others or nature. Historic, systemic, and intergenerational trauma compound this stress, changing our minds, bodies, and energies in ways we are only beginning to discover.

Trauma is a shared experience across all of humanity, yet we have been slow to grasp its nature and presence and, as a species, we are trapped by the trauma of our survival. We have species-level trauma memories encoded in our DNA. Even if we don't carry the personal memories, we carry a memorial to brutality and domination stored in our cells. The adage "those who don't learn from history are doomed to repeat it" should read "are doomed to *relive* it." We don't learn from history because we don't just remember it, we relive it—much as people who suffer from PTSD and other trauma-related illnesses constantly relive what happened to them.

Our unacknowledged, unintegrated, unreleased past keeps us trapped, preying on and harming each other.

We didn't know before but we do now—if we are going to be more and do more than survive, we have to change how we think about our choices and how we make them; we have to think, feel, and act beyond the radius of immediate circumstance. Making such visionary, evolutionary change demands the hard work of accessing ourselves in new ways;

DOI: 10.4324/9781003048312-6

moving beyond the instinct for survival at any cost. We have to *want* to be more than apex predators headed toward extinction.

We have to *want* to learn and grow and imagine new genres of choices, life-affirming choices. We have the ability to choose beyond the animal's instinct to survive, as we learn from Pinker (2012), but we cannot do that while we are trapped in endless cycles of trauma. Our ability to learn and integrate that learning is key to creating and making life-affirming choices.

Repurposing Education

I started teaching in a community-based organization where I taught basic computer skills to adults during the mid-1990s. This was in the early days of desktop computing, and I didn't have easy access to prepared curricula or teaching tips. At that time, I had no formal training in education or teaching, nor was I prepared to work with students with multiple barriers to learning—I had no idea such barriers existed. I learned everything on the job, from writing curricula and lesson plans, rudimentary program design, to finding out the hard way not to assume prior learning or knowledge. I realized quickly that my students needed to learn how to learn if they were going to get through the class, let alone use their new skills in the workplace.

I maintained this approach throughout my career, even when teaching traditional college courses that offer little room for such a time-intensive approach. Looking back, I realize I was trying to ensure no one would feel left behind or shamed—a difficult thing to do inside the constraints of organized education. Teaching in prison was when I more fully explored the benefits of closely attending to individual learning needs; when I recognized the importance of developing curiosity and self-confidence. With few exceptions, my students needed considerable time to strengthen their belief in themselves as learners before I could begin content-specific teaching.

I am not alone in this experience.

Most adult educators I know, especially those who work with students labeled as needing the most help have had similar experiences. English language learners, refugees, immigrants, first generation in a family to attend college, historically underrepresented populations, poor students, and people with disabilities—these are the people organized education, at all levels, has failed and continues to fail.

Teachers scramble to teach enough of an invisible "learn how to learn" curriculum so they can turn around and hammer away on content, hoping students can immediately use unfamiliar learning skills. The pace is rushed, teachers and students alike feeling like they are missing out, but are not entirely sure what they are missing. Whenever I talk with these teachers and students, faces light up as they remember the moments they felt most connected—to themselves and others. They remember most the moments of an expanded, connected learning state, similar to extended lightbulb moments.

As with other Euro-white systems, organized education was not born of a collective, collaborative, shared dream of who we might be and become. This lack of creative organization has never been addressed and so education drifts and decays, waiting for us to bring it new meaning and purpose.

Repurposing education is not about changing outcomes, it is about opening our perception so that measurable outcomes are not the only priority. In the larger view, such a change demands that we consider what kind of learners we want to create, and that we move in that direction with deliberation and thoughtfulness. Repurposing corrections education, specifically, means that students reclaim themselves as learners, not just as participants in vocational or academic programs.

The Expansive Learning model offers a way into that reimagining; a way to reorient toward ourselves as curious beings who long to know more about ourselves, others, our planet, and how best to serve and sustain life.

The Expansive Learning Model

The Expansive Learning Model (ELM) reframes the purpose of education as expansion, rebalancing learning through and across four Elements in a cycle. It describes how I experience and teach the learning process—as a cycle with discrete, but interdependent elements. These elements address four unique aspects of learning, and every person is capable of learning in each element (Figure 6.1).

What I find compelling about this model is that it is non-linear and non-binary—there is no "end" to learning and more than one way to enter and move through the process. Teachers and learners both can move phases in and out of focus as necessary, depending on what is being taught and what the learner needs. The model becomes a tool for teaching learners about their own learning process and placing ultimate control over their learning into their hands. Teaching people *how* to learn changes how we approach education by

- Focusing on learning how to learn as a worthwhile and necessary endeavor in itself.
- Redistributing learning across Elements, reducing the emphasis on content.
- Providing learners with a map to discovering their own learning process.
- Equalizing the responsibility for learning across teacher, student, process, and content.
- Redefining "strong learning" to encompass skills in all four elements.

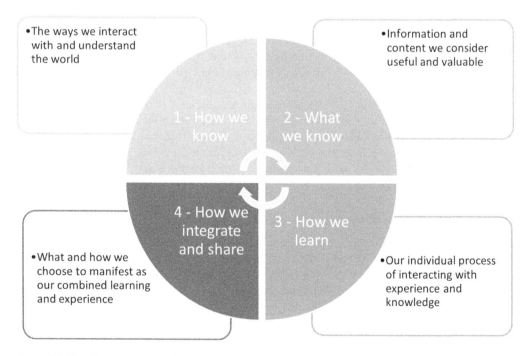

Figure 6.1 The Expansive Learning Model.

Source: Daniels, M (2020), Spokane WA. Copyright (2020) by M. Daniels. Reprinted with permission.

I encourage you to think about how you can share your learning with students. Go through the ELM with them, share the Trauma-Responsive Framework, and how you have incorporated it into your teaching practice. Learning together is revolutionary practice—a direct challenge to Dominator dynamics and content supremacy. For any of us to truly grasp that what happened to us does not define us, that we have agency over how we use our hearts and minds to learn and grow, despite all the harm our learning self has endured, is a liberating experience, no matter the environment.

When creating this model, I leaned into the practical, seeking a map that could apply across frameworks, learning styles, and preferences. While there are similarities and parallels to other learning models, the focus on the process of learning is broadly inclusive of multiple styles and methods. Let's look at each Element more closely.

Element 1 - How We Know

How we know the world is our most basic framework of understanding and making meaning. Nichols' framework gives us one set of examples of this knowing, based on large groupings of culture and ethnicity. The "how" of our knowing is rarely addressed, although cultural competency has been a topic of discussion for decades. Organized education in the United States expends massive resources in its attempts to force learning through Euro-white frameworks, with little regard or acknowledgment that other frameworks exist. Teaching students through their own frameworks, or even that other frameworks exist is the first step in liberating them as learners.

Element 2 - What We Know

What we know encompasses all the knowledge we consider useful and vital to our experience and survival. All people and cultures have specific bodies and collections of knowledge and knowing they value, share, protect, and add to, and the "how" of knowing is often embedded in the "what" of knowledge. Groups may share some of these ways of learning and types of knowledge, but much is unique and tied to the factors that contribute to a shared ethnic or racial heritage.

In the United States, organized education prizes this Element above all others, as it aligns well with accumulation and quantification of intellectual expertise. Education systems explicitly focus on what we know, while implicitly requiring that that knowledge be taught, consumed, and acted upon in Euro-white culturally specific ways only. In this way, content expertise is invisibly merged with Euro-white cultural competency, a toxic pairing that undergirds organized education.

Element 3 - How We Learn

How we learn encompasses all the different ways we interact with, consume, and retain knowledge. This is where we would consider individual learning styles, specific accessibility needs, environmental factors, individual/group dynamics, teacher/student relationships, classroom and environment, pedagogy and andragogy, and all the other factors that go into teaching and learning.

Organized education in the United States expends considerable resources researching how we learn, as individuals. This is a necessary component of any educational endeavor, but individual needs are a combination of the personal and the cultural. Exploring only what we need as individuals, without taking cultural context into account, provides an incomplete and inaccurate map to fully integrated learning.

Element 4 - How We Integrate and Share

How we integrate and share is a two-part process in which we transform raw data into lived experience and wisdom. Like Element 1, it is neglected in US educational systems. Without this Element, our learning cycle is incomplete. Naming this overlooked aspect of learning calls attention to its importance beyond consideration as a preference or a learning style.

Service learning and intern/externships are examples of integrating learning, although they rarely require sharing beyond a paper or class presentation. Mentoring programs of all types are examples of how we share what we've learned, but it is not always clear whether the mentor has truly integrated, or is trying to integrate, what they share with their mentees. For example, I have seen any number of mentor/mentee relationships in which the mentor shares how they solved a particular type of problem, or got through a hard time, not what they learned or how their decision making and problem solving have changed.

While the details of how the mentor handled a situation might be important or interesting, it is unclear whether they have reflected upon their own learning process, and put that reflected learning to work in their own lives. If we include integration and sharing as part of a robust aspect of the learning cycle, reflection on multiple layers of learning can occur more naturally.

Elements 1 and 4 are crucial elements I have rarely seen in education, although they do show up from time to time. Most often, they are treated as a special type of content expertise, occasionally as "non-traditional learning," but never have I seen them incorporated as fully integrated aspects of a robust learning cycle. Most of us are intimately familiar with Elements 2 and 3, as they constitute the vast majority of our educational resources and knowledge. Challenging ourselves—as teachers—to become learners again is not an easy or comfortable proposition.

As we increase our awareness of our own learning process, we will start to feel the gaps, and without care, our discomfort with knowledge gaps will quickly turn to shame, anger, and defeat. But by this point, you should have a network of colleagues and practitioners you can turn to for support, as well as remembering to extend grace to yourself. What I love most about this model is that using it places teachers in the role of learners, oftentimes with their students. I can't imagine a better way to discard the illusion of organized education, and actively dismantle and rebuild its structure than by becoming an expansive learner *with* your students, and with other teacher-learners.

Expansive learning is based in relationship, curiosity, and freedom to grow, where organized education prizes transaction, conformation, and content expertise. Organized education, at its worst, partners easily with other rigid systems of control. Public education has long been the primary source for educating the working poor and middle class, and many of its practices reinforce these same traits—transaction, conformity, and content expertise. Even with preparation, every prison educator committed to creating space for expansive learning is likely to encounter suspicion, resistance, and resentment.

Shift and Rebalance

The instinctive desire to survive—at a species level—is hardwired in ways we need—all life wants to survive. But our evolution cannot continue to be based solely on the survival of our physical selves, although we are brilliantly brutal in its pursuit (Emergent Strategy, 2017, p. 6). brown also envisions and works toward our realignment, a future born of shared dignity, expansion, and movement into balance, all of which are profoundly connected with both the Framework and ELM.

Our most thoughtful, creative, and compassionate activists, organizers, mystics, and thought leaders say without doubt or hesitation that unacknowledged and unresolved trauma causes profound isolation and, simultaneously, severely compromises our natural tendence and ability toward connection. Expansive learning and tending to trauma do not disregard survival, but evolve our conception of surviving beyond domination and predation. They are a movement toward using our higher consciousness to survive instead of the destruction that is our legacy.

Look at any set of "best practices" in trauma work and note that the top two are about piercing the veil of isolation and offering safety in connection. In our context as learners, this approach—focusing on connection and our shared humanity and environment—is a personal, cultural, and spiritual rebalancing. Placing this rebalancing into the context of leaners and vibrant learning spaces leads us toward integration; making-meaning of our traumatic experience and choosing how that meaning informs our awareness and presence in the world.

Death row attorney Bryan Stevenson, author of *Just Mercy* (2015), in an interview with Keosha Varela, provides clear direction for those who choose the harder path to justice:

> **Get closer to the issues:** too many people try to problem solve from a distance and that distance means you miss details and nuance, limiting the effectiveness of solutions
>
> **Change the narrative:** this happens when we speak clearly and directly to the issue of race, its history in the US. We must acknowledge the damage inflicted through the genocide of Native people, slavery of African people, Jim Crow, and now mass incarceration and embedded structures of oppression.
>
> **Fight against hopelessness, "the enemy of justice":** Hope keeps us standing and speaking when others sit or are quiet.
>
> **Get uncomfortable:** Being human means suffering. Becoming familiar with our own pain and suffering gives us courage to be present with the suffering of others, regardless of our discomfort (Four Ways to Help Bend the Moral Arc of the Universe toward Justice, n.d.).

Entering teaching as trauma-responsive practice presses into each of these directions, challenging the heart of our self-image as successful teachers, as helpers, as caring people. We are trained to impatience with learning; to harry those who do not interact with the world through the Euro-white knowledgescape. In a system that rejects nuance, even the most open-minded of us think rigidly about teaching outcomes, and what a "good" learning process and environment should be. The ELM provides a way to revision the learning process, while the Framework provides an example of how we might structure that process.

This work, in the context of learning is integration and rebalance; building expansive learners—students who are aware of themselves as learners and have control over their learning process. Freire (1972) and Lorde (2020) both have stated, emphatically, that we cannot restore our humanity by using the oppressor's methods, and that neither dehumanization nor full humanity remain constant.

Balance and realignment could include the entire spectrum of trauma-responsivity; acknowledging our trauma, integrating that learning, releasing pain, then continue exploring our multi-faceted, creative selves. These two states, which are both necessary and valuable, exist in a learning spectrum that has just begun revealing itself.

Framework + Model

Expansive learning, combined with trauma-responsive practice changes both theory and practice, opening us toward entirely new horizons. And this is what we do differently—we change the tools and the structure by changing their composition and purpose. We change how we are in the world and the world changes. The Framework is a tool, meant to be used, tested, improved on, and incorporated into your own teaching style and ability. How you use it and your understanding of its place and shape should transform, as your own experience and practice grow and shift.

The Points of Entry diagram presents education as a legitimate pathway into trauma work, but only if organized education can change. If education is to become liberatory, and we truly desire that our ability to learn be turned to a greater purpose, the nature and purpose of education must also change.

Education and Healing

Throughout this text, I have been emphatic that "healing" is too broad a term, and that education serves a different purpose in addressing trauma than our current definition of healing. Shawn Ginwright, in an article on the future of healing, writes about Healing Centered Engagement (HCE) as "tectonic shift in how we view trauma, its causes, and intervention. HCE is strength based, advances a collective view of healing, and re-centers culture as a central feature in well-being" (2018). Ginwright and others defining a strengths-based approach present an excellent point—people are more than what has happened to them.

As we continue to evolve our thinking and language around these large, intricate topics, it is worthwhile to reiterate that whatever our role, the only person we are truly responsible for healing and caring for is ourselves. Even within our internal caregiving, we should consider our language carefully. Palmer tells us that "[t]he human soul does not want to be fixed, it wants simply to be seen and heard" (2010, p. 152), and how that needs to happen is different for everyone.

Scott, Warber, & Dieppe provide a qualitative look at what trauma recovery and healing can encompass, also noting that each person's recovery is quite individual. In their study, participants experienced an incredible range and depth of healing journeys including overcoming terrifying events to become healers, to people finding ways to manage their daily lives with serious health concerns.

"The degree and quality of suffering experienced by each individual is framed by contextual factors…In the healing journey, bridges from suffering are developed to healing resources/skills and connections to helpers outside themselves… From the iteration between suffering and developing resources and connections, a new state emerges that involves hope, self-acceptance and helping others (2017)."

There is no journey to recovery or healing that does not involve learning, and a strong ability to learn may become one of our greatest tools for healing.

Learning Ourselves into Joy

Rebecca Solnit (2004) and Pema Chodron (2000, 2007) both speak of abandoning a particular type of hope: an abstract dream of something better, a return to familiarity, less discomfort, and out of our direct responsibility.

That type of hope, which is a form of inattention, has taken a severe blow and it is a gift that we can now create a new kind of hope—a hope that is, like true nonviolence, grounded in active, assertive love for self and others. hooks (2001) and Dr. King, Jr. (1963, 1967) both identified this love and called us to its purpose—to affirm life and act with firm intention; to create and grow a world where all life is cared for and about.

Part of our journey is to understand that resolving and releasing our trauma is about evolution. We are at a point in our existence as a species where—for possibly the first time—we can make a conscious choice about who we want to be, how we want to grow. We can choose to affirm life by acknowledging our personal traumatic histories (known and unknown, conscious and unconscious, genetic and societal), working toward wholeness, partnering and encouraging others to do the same.

Perhaps the greatest gift we receive from a deeper understanding of the nature and impacts of trauma is that we can begin to sense and reach for the core, the essence, of our students. We can use that core element of who they are to sense and hold space for its emergence and growth. By honoring and encouraging that truest piece of them, we can make it safe for them to be brave and do the same for themselves and each other. Even in the darkest of environments, we can seek this truth.

Facing and acknowledging trauma is the shift we must make to evolve. If trauma changes our biology (ETH Zurich, 2014) and thus our DNA (Cantor, 2009; Christopher, 2004), then healing, recovering from, or resolving our trauma may do the same. If we evolve partly through our response to trauma, then accepting and addressing traumatic experiences, current or historical, may offer us a way to participate in our own evolution as a species—in a positive, creative way. With integration and balance informing our purpose, we can redirect our exploration of learning to include compelling new visions for our future.

In Washington, there is a group of educators working on a project titled "Constellations for Decolonizing: Leading with Racial Equity," an effort "…to imagine an aspirational, iterative, multi-dimensional, constellations framework that seeks healing, *umoja* reunification of body, mind, spirit, to one another and the land, as well as transformative justice" (brown, 2017), and "targeting the root causes of racism, and attempts to defy time and space" (Martinez, Howell-Williams, Forero, Neider, Tuncap, Chin, Jimenez, Rodriguez, Richardson, Whetham, Barrington 2020).

From that work, we look to people's comfort in their own bodies, their connection to other people, and their awareness of their place on the land and in the world as learning outcomes. Or we listen to Darnell Moore and seek capacity and willingness for self-reflection; to strive for emotional intelligence and maturity (2019). Ross Gay writes about tending joy and practicing delight, and seeking community in luminous moments (2020). Jonathan Rowson speaks to a subtle awakening of consciousness, that we may need to redefine or rediscover who we are (2019), and Amichai Lau-Lavie imagines and explores "…containers of we…," that are a crucial "…first aid for spiritual seekers who are very, very thirsty" (2017).

All of these require proximity, a closeness that trauma short–circuits until it is tended. Any or all of these could be placed in the context of expansive learning, emboldening us to redefine ourselves as teachers and learners.

Teaching is an extension of expansive learning, and teachers must re-become learners. That is why improv is such a useful skill—it is a way to organize an unexpected opening to teach and learn simultaneously. The best moments I have ever had as a teacher are when I learn something at the same time as my students. I may not be learning the same thing, but we are learning together. This happens when joy is present, and joy makes this shared learning possible. A commitment to expansive learning turns us in a life-affirming direction, reimagining joy in adult learning spaces.

If fear contracts the nervous system, joy expands it. Joy is an emotional expression of love, of care, and fear cannot remain when joy is present. No matter the circumstances or environment, you can teach with joy and fear subsides, even if only for a moment. I imagine and feel joy as an antidote to trauma, perhaps one of many, but one that must be reconnected with learning and teaching both. Bringing joy into the bleakness of prison allows us to be present with the pain of others and accept them and ourselves as fully human. Where fear is greatest joy can be greatest, as joy emerges from facing and embracing the shared experience of being human.

References

brown, a. m. (2017). *Emergent strategy*. Chico, CA: AK Press.

Cantor, C. (2009). Post-traumatic stress disorder: Evolutionary perspectives. *Australian & New Zealand Journal of Psychiatry*, *43*(11), 1038–1048. doi:10.3109/00048670903270407. PMID: 20001399.

Chodron, P. (2000). *When things fall apart*. Boston, MA: Shambhala Publications.

Chodron, P. (2007). *The places that scare you*. Boston, MA: Shambhala Publications.

Christopher, M. (2004). A broader view of trauma: A biopsychosocial-evolutionary view of the role of the traumatic stress response in the emergence of pathology and/or growth. *Clinical Psychology Review*, *24*(1), 75–98. doi:10.1016/j.cpr.2003.12.003

ETH Zurich. (2014). *Hereditary trauma: Inheritance of traumas and how they may be mediated*. Retrieved from https://www.sciencedaily.com/releases/2014/04/140413135953.htm

Freire, P. (1972). *Pedagogy of the oppressed*. New York, Herder and Herder.

Gay, R. (2020). Tending joy and practicing delight. *On being with Krista Tippett*. (K. Tippett, Interviewer) Retrieved from https://onbeing.org/programs/ross-gay-tending-joy-and-practicing-delight/

Ginwright, S. (2018). *The future of healing: Shifting from trauma informed care to healing centered engagement*. Retrieved from https://ginwright.medium.com/the-future-of-healing-shifting-from-trauma-informed-care-to-healing-centered-engagement-634f557ce69c

hooks, b. (2001). *All about love*. New York, NY: Harper Collins.

King, M. L. (1963). *Strength to love*. Philadelphia, PA: Fortress Press.

King, M. L. (1967). *Where do we go from here*. New York, NY: Harper & Row Publishing.

Lau-Lavie, A. (2017). First aid for spiritual seekers. *On being with Krista Tippett*. (K. Tippett, Interviewer). Retrieved from https://onbeing.org/programs/amichai-lau-lavie-first-aid-for-spiritual-seekers/

Lorde, A. (1984). *Sister outsider*. New York, NY: Crossing Press.

Martinez, A., Hohwell-Williams, V., Forero, C.,   Neider, X., Tuncap, M., Chin, A., Jimenez, M., Rodriguez, Y., Richardson, C., Whetham, J., Barrington, M., (2020). *Draft 1 Constellations for decolonizing: Leading with racial equity* (In Progress, unpublished). Retrieved from https://docs.google.com/document/d/1ecpqM2dp3tmKAX4ek9a_cv01F8pclcKSxEkxoX8mBLw/edit

Moore, D. (2019). Self-reflection and social evolution. *On being with Krista Tippett*. (K. Tippett, Interviewer). Retrieved from https://onbeing.org/programs/darnell-moore-self-reflection-and-social-evolution/

Palmer, P. J. (2010). *The courage to teach: Exploring the inner landscape of a teacher's life*. Hoboken, NY: Wiley.

Pinker, S. (2012). *The better angels of our nature*. New York, NY: Penguin Group.

Rowson, J. (2019. Integrating our souls, systems, and society. *On being with Krista Tippett*. (K. Tippett, Interviewer). Retrieved from https://onbeing.org/programs/jonathan-rowson-integrating-our-souls-systems-and-society/

Scott, J., Warber, S., & Dieppe P. E. A. (2017). Healing journey: A qualitative analysis of the healing experiences of Americans suffering from trauma and illness. *BMJ Open*, 7, e016771. DOI: 10.1136/bmjopen-2017-016771

Solnit, R. (2004). *Hope in the dark*. Chicago, IL: Haymarket Books.

Stevenson, B. (2015). *Just mercy*. New York, NY: One World/Ballantine.

Stevenson, B. (2017). *Four ways to help bend the moral arc of the universe toward justice*. Retrieved from https://www.educationpioneers.org/blog/four-ways-help-bend-moral-arc-universe-toward-justice

Chapter 7

Learning Outward

Organized education in the United States has become a system of oppression that strikes to the core of our humanity. It limits our understanding about and knowledge of the world to one cultural perspective, teaching us that there is only that one perspective. This approach has narrowed our hearts and minds so that we are culturally, emotionally, and intellectually out of balance. As a consequence, we are losing our ability to embrace change in a rapidly changing world.

Such a large part of who we are, individually and collectively, arises from how we learn about and experience the world. We are shaped by everything that touches us and we can learn from that touch, and use that learning to change ourselves and influence the world.

Our ability to learn is the keystone to this endeavor.

When our learning is constrained primarily in service to survival, we cannot express our creative self to its fullest extent. Expanding our thinking about traumatic experience reveals new ways to consider its impacts and antidotes; tend harm and offer healing; acknowledge and integrate what we have learned.

Repurposing education can provide a pathway to settling the body and expanding the nervous system, and the Trauma-Responsive Framework and Expansive Learning Model are tools for this repurposing. Trauma-responsive education strengthens ability to learn, in part through skills and experiences that directly counter the impacts of trauma.

The Expansive Learning Model reshapes our approach to education through cultural rebalancing, fully integrating learning via sharing and reflection, and changing the intent of education to developing generous and imaginative learners. Both of these approaches invite adult educators to reframe themselves as learners, rediscover the joy of learning, and share that joy with students.

Adult educators are not often encouraged toward joy in teaching or learning. While teaching itself can be a joyful endeavor, that pleasure is overshadowed by system demands, complex student needs, and our personal fears and doubts in the face of so many obstacles to learning. Teaching people *how* to learn, instead of teaching only *what* to learn, gives adult educators a fresh vision of teaching and learning, for themselves and their students.

Belief in ourselves as creative, expressive, learning beings moves us in a life-affirming direction. It is the seed we need to grow and nurture a future that is the fullest expression of our best selves.

In grace, joy, and solidarity,

em

DOI: 10.4324/9781003048312-7

Index

Made in United States
North Haven, CT
23 December 2021

13533370R00089